1st & 2nd Timothy and Titus

The Final Letters

Linda Osborne

Copyright © 2016 Linda Osborne. All rights reserved.

Unless otherwise noted, all Scripture quotations are from the NEW AMERICAN STANDARD BIBLE®, Copyright © 1960, 1962, 1963, 1968, 1971, 1972, 1973, 1975, 1977, 1995 by The Lockman Foundation. Used by permission.

Published by Catch the Vision! Press
909 E Palm Avenue, Redlands, CA 92374

ISBN-10: 0692528989
ISBN-13: 978-0692528983

OTHER BOOKS/BIBLE STUDIES BY THE AUTHOR

Called to Lead: Catch the Vision!
Acts: Church Alive!
Colossians: Christ Supreme
David: Shepherd of Israel
Ephesians: Blessed!
Galatians: Born (again!) to Be Free
Genesis: Beginnings
James: Let's Grow Up!
John: The Gospel of the Beloved
Philippians: Unrestrained Joy!
Revelation: Seven Letters to Seven Churches
Romans: The Gospel According to Paul
Ruth: A Love Story
The Women: Part One
and
Lunch-Hour Lessons: Revelation

CONTENTS

	Preface	i
1	1 Timothy 1	Pg 1
2	1 Timothy 2	Pg 14
3	1 Timothy 3	Pg 28
4	1 Timothy 4	Pg 42
5	1 Timothy 5	Pg 56
6	1 Timothy 6	Pg 69
7	2 Timothy 1	Pg 83
8	2 Timothy 2	Pg 98
9	2 Timothy 3	Pg 113
10	2 Timothy 4	Pg 127
11	Titus 1	Pg 142
12	Titus 2	Pg 156
13	Titus 3	Pg 170
	About the Author	Pg 184

PREFACE

Letters ... we love to get them don't we? But what about a letter from your mentor, your father in the faith: the one who led you to Christ and led you into ministry? Even better! Well that's what we have in these letters to Timothy and Titus: the final letters written by Paul.

While it is uncertain of the exact nature of events, it seems most likely that Paul wrote these letters after being released from his first imprisonment in Rome. 1 Timothy was written from Macedonia around AD 64 to Timothy, who had been left to supervise the church at Ephesus. Titus, in the same manner, had been left at Crete to oversee the churches there. Paul probably wrote to him from Macedonia (or possibly Nicopolis) sometime after he wrote his first letter to Timothy. Paul's final letter to Timothy (*Paul's final letter*) was written from Rome, about AD 66 or 67 during his second and last imprisonment, and shortly before he was beheaded.

Although these letters were written at different times, from different locations, to two different men, the message is the same. Paul wanted Timothy and Titus to continue in the faith and carry out the duties he had left them. We almost see him passing the baton--the mantel of authority, as his own time of ministry was about to end.

Well today, *we* continue the ministry of Paul to build up the body of Christ and to take the good news to a world that needs Him. So let's take hold of the baton as it is passed our way and *take it personally*!

1 TIMOTHY 1

Day 1
Read 1 Timothy 1, concentrating on verses 1-2

1. By what title of authority does Paul identify himself in verse 1a?

The word apostle comes from the Greek word *apostolos*, which means, *one who is sent.* In a general way, this title was used by many who were sent out in the name of Jesus, but, in specific, it was the title given to those closest to Jesus—the 12 disciples who were chosen to take the message of Jesus Christ to the world. Although Paul was not a part of that original group, he was given a special commission by Jesus Christ Himself.

   a. Scan Acts 9:1-20 for the amazing conversion of Saul/Paul on his way to Damascus.

   b. How does Paul describe himself in contrast to the other apostles? 1 Corinthians 15:7-9

We will be considering Paul's testimony further in the third day of our lesson.

2. By whose authority did Paul call himself an apostle? v. 1

   a. How would Paul's authority as apostle give Timothy's word strength as he instructed the churches according to Paul's direction? (Remember, Timothy was left at Ephesus by Paul as *his* representative.)

3. In this address to Timothy, what did Paul call Timothy? v. 2

   a. Obviously, Paul was not Timothy's father—what do you imagine this meant?

It is understood that Timothy came to faith during Paul's first missionary journey.

   b. 2 Timothy 1:5 and 3:15 give us background on Timothy's upbringing. Share what you learn about him from these verses.

c. Acts 16:1-3 describes how Timothy came to serve with Paul on Paul's second missionary journey. List the various things you learn about Timothy from these verses.

Timothy had a very important role in Paul's ministry. One interesting fact is that Timothy was with Paul when he wrote Romans, 2 Corinthians, 1 Thessalonians, Philippians, and Philemon.

4. In what four ways did Paul speak of God and His Son Jesus Christ in these first two verses?

   a. How might these terms have been a specific encouragement to Timothy in his highly responsible position at Ephesus?

   b. In verse 2, Paul speaks three words of blessing upon Timothy. Beside each word write a dictionary definition (which would pertain to its meaning in this context), or simply what *you* understand it to mean:

   ⚜ *grace*—

✤ *mercy—*

✤ *peace—*

   c. Which one of these three blessings do you most need in your life today? Won't you bow your heart and ask Him to pour this blessing out upon you?

5. 1 Corinthians 4:17 and Philippians 2:19-22 give us an intimate glimpse of Paul's heart toward Timothy and the value he placed on his ministry. From these verses, write a statement of Paul's relationship with this special young man.

It is not insignificant that the final letter written by Paul was written to his dear friend Timothy.

This week's memory verse: "But the goal of our instruction is love from a pure heart and a good conscience and a sincere faith." 1 Timothy 1:5

1st Timothy 1

Day 2
Read 1 Timothy 1:3-11

1. As Paul left Ephesus for Macedonia, verse 3 explains his primary purpose for leaving Timothy there. What was it?

   a. What is doctrine? In simple terms, what would you consider a "strange doctrine" to be?

Paul had foreseen many years earlier the potential for this very problem.

2. Recorded in Acts 20:28-30 are Paul's parting words to the elders of the church at Ephesus, after having been with them for a period of three years. What was his warning to them?

   a. The following verses give us a sampling of Paul's instruction on the subject of false teachers and false teaching. What does he say?

   ✢ Romans 16:17

   ✢ 1 Timothy 4:7

✣ 1 Timothy 6:3-4a

✣ 2 Timothy 2:14

✣ 2 Timothy 4:3-4

b. What is Paul's clear pronouncement upon the teaching of any other gospel message? Galatians 1:8-9

The New Testament is this *gospel* which we have received. Any teaching we receive, if it is not in line with what we learn in Matthew, Mark, Luke, John, Acts, Romans, etc., must be discerned as useless, false, and harmful to our very faith, and must be rejected completely.

3. In 1 Timothy 1:3-7, Paul points out four ways in which these false teachers err in their teaching. What are they?

verse 3

verse 4a

verse 6

verse 7

a. Were the teachings and discussions of these men bringing people closer to the truth of the gospel? What does verse 4 say?

Paul understood, better than any, the simple truth of the gospel message. The false teachers were distorting the simple message of grace and faith.

4. What clear statement did Paul make about the law in verse 8?

   a. Speaking generally of the *law*, who does Paul say law is <u>not</u> made for? v. 9

   b. Who *is* the law made for? vv. 9-10 (You may make a list.)

The words, "whatever is contrary to sound teaching, according to the glorious gospel of the blessed God" (v. 10 NASB), is a help to us here. Those who lived by the sound, healthy, wholesome teaching of the gospel were a law unto themselves—abiding by the teachings of their Lord. It was only those who lived by that which was contrary to the pure gospel message that needed to be brought under law.

It seems that the false teaching in Ephesus was leading those who were *free in Christ* back into bondage. It was leading to fruitless discussions, wasting valuable time with that which was not only untrue but also useless and which gave rise to "mere speculation, rather than furthering the administration of God *which is by faith*."

5. In contrast to the false teaching, what does Paul say was the purpose of the instruction to which *they* (he and Timothy) were committed? v. 5

The true gospel message would be given *in* love from a pure heart and a good conscience and a sincere faith and would, in turn, *produce* love, *and* a pure heart, *and* a good conscience *and* a sincere faith! Paul also wanted to encourage Timothy that the work he would undertake to correct the false teachers would result only in *good* for them *and* for those who had been listening to their message.

Review this week's memory verse.

Day 3
Read 1 Timothy 1:12-20

Paul now turns for a moment and reminisces over the mercy extended to him by his gracious Lord and Savior. In his own personal testimony to the grace of Christ, we see the gospel message in its truest form.

1. According to verse 12, what two things did Jesus do for Paul?

a. Paul says that Jesus put him into the ministry—*although*—although what? v. 13

b. Acts 8:1-3 describes Saul/Paul at the time Stephen was martyred for his Christianity. How does it portray him?

c. And yet, in what manner did Jesus act toward Paul? (1 Timothy 1:13) Why?

2. See Acts 9:1-20 again for Paul's encounter with Christ. Why was it merciful for Jesus Christ to save Paul in the way He did?

a. Remember for a moment *your* testimony before Christ saved you. How was it merciful of Jesus Christ to save *you*?

3. Why did Jesus come into the world, according to Paul's testimony? v. 15

Notice how Paul sees himself, perhaps you see yourself in the very same way.

a. How was Paul—who was called to serve (verse 12)—able to go forward in his new faith and not allow his past to hinder him? Philippians 3:12-14

b. What does 2 Corinthians 5:17 tell us that helps us see why Paul was able to go forward?

Perhaps you need to take heart to this same truth—that you are a new creature in Christ and that the old things have passed away. Don't allow Satan to keep you in bondage to your past—let Paul be your example. Forgetting what lies behind, reach forward to what lies ahead!

4. What does Paul consider the reason he was given the mercy of Jesus Christ? v. 16

a. *Digging Deeper:* Verse 17 is considered to be a typical doxology (a hymn or verse of praise to God) given by Paul as a natural response to his experience of God's mercy. Can you understand why Paul would speak so highly of the one who saved him, *the chief of sinners*? Would you like to write your own doxology of praise and thanksgiving to God *your* Savior?

5. What threefold word of exhortation—actually a command—did Paul give Timothy in the closing verses of chapter 1? vv. 18-19

   a. Look ahead to 2 Timothy 4:6-8, and see how these very words became the final written testimony of the great apostle Paul. (It's not too early to consider what you would like your final testimony, at the end of your life on this earth, to be.)

Review this week's memory verse.

Day 4
Overview of 1 Timothy 1

Today we will be looking at the passage we have studied this week as a whole. The goal is to find the main lessons the Lord has for us from this chapter. Don't worry about being clever or profound—just do your best!

Find the Facts ...
1. See if you can state the *content* of this week's passage in a couple of sentences. (Who is speaking, what is taking place, what is the main subject?)

Look for the Heart...

2. What do you think is the main *lesson* of this passage? (What spiritual truths are taught here? Is there a command to obey, a warning to heed, a promise to claim?)

Hear Him Speak...

3. Look for a *personal application* from the content of this passage. It should come from the lesson you got from the chapter (question 2). How will you apply the lesson to yourself?

4. Was there a particular verse that ministered to you this week? What was it and how did it minister to you?

5. Write out your memory verse *from memory*!

NOTES

1 TIMOTHY 2

In chapter 1, Paul laid the foundation for Timothy's difficult ministry in Ephesus. We may see chapter 1 as introductory in the sense that all that follows hinges upon it. Paul is instructing Timothy on how to guide this particular church, which is being confused and misled by false teaching. We must keep this in mind as we study the verses that follow. It may be said that chapter 2 actually begins the main subject of this letter, which is held by most to be *behaving in the house of God:* "... I write so that you may know how you ought to conduct yourself in the house of God ..." (1 Timothy 3:15). Let us read all that follows with the desire to gain God's perspective on how we are to live as Christians.

Day 1
Read 1 Timothy 2:1-8

Paul's first order of instruction concerns worship—in particular, prayer.

1. What are the four words Paul uses for prayer in verse 1?

1st Timothy 2

Rather than simply speaking of four *types* of prayer, these words give a picture of the scope of prayer.

    a. Consider your time of prayer. Do your personal prayers include these elements? See if you can share your thoughts on some of the different aspects of prayer, using these words of Paul.

    b. Who are we to pray for, according to this verse?

2. Who, specifically, does Paul mention that prayers be offered for in verse 2? For what purpose?

At the time this was written, the emperor Nero was in authority. He was a cruel ruler and persecution for Christians was growing.

    a. What does Romans 13:1 say on this subject?

    b. What does 1 Peter 2:13-14 say?

    c. In what way is Paul's command in 1 Timothy 2:1-2 on a higher level than these other verses?

d. What can you learn from Paul's words to Timothy that you can apply today?

3. Why is it good to pray for others—even our enemies—according to verses 3-4?

   a. How many people does God wish to come to the knowledge of the truth? How does 2 Peter 3:9b say this?

4. *Digging Deeper:* Verse 5 tells us there is one God and that His Son Jesus Christ is the one Mediator between God and men. Look at the following verses and share your understanding of who Christ is and why He alone is that Mediator: John 1:1, 14; Philippians 2:5-7; Hebrews 4:14-15.

5. What did this God-Man, Jesus Christ, do for us? v. 6 (You may also see Philippians 2:8.)

   a. What does it mean to be a ransom? (You may want to look the word up in your dictionary.)

b. For how many was Jesus Christ a ransom? What does John 12:32 say about this?

The key word in this passage is *all*. We are to pray for *all* men (v. 1), because God desires *all* to be saved (v. 4), so much so that He sent His Son Jesus Christ to be a ransom for *all* (v. 6).

c. Do *all* avail themselves of the sacrifice made on their behalf? What do you think about that?

Paul says it was for this very purpose—to proclaim this very message—that he was appointed a preacher, an apostle, and a teacher of the Gentiles, in faith and truth. Up until now it was understood that the Messiah was coming only to save the Jews. That was actually a *mis*understanding. Jesus Christ came to save *all* men! (You may see God's original promise to Abraham in Genesis 12:1-3.)

Therefore, Paul says, he wants the men in every place to pray ... (v. 8 NASB).

6. How were they to pray? v. 8

The lifting up of holy hands signifies reverence and submission to God. Praying without wrath and doubting (or dissension) is necessary to have our prayers heard and answered. This was likely one of the problems in the church at Ephesus.

a. Has this passage given you any new insight into prayer (who to pray for, why to pray, and that God is in full agreement with your prayers for the salvation of others)? Share any new or important thoughts you may have.

Paul specifically mentions the men in verse 8. In these 8 verses, Paul was speaking to the men in the church whose role it was to publicly offer up prayers.

This week's memory verse: "But I want you to understand that Christ is the head of every man, and the man is the head of a woman, and God is the head of Christ." 1 Corinthians 11:3

Day 2
Read 1 Timothy 2:9-10

Paul begins verse 9 with the words, "in like manner" (NKJV) or "likewise" (NASB). Verse 9 is actually a continuation of verse 8, although Paul is now directing his words to the women in the church.

1. What, again, were the two conditions Paul laid down for men as they led public prayer meetings in the church? v. 8

    a. The lifting up of the hands was a common posture for prayer. What do you think Paul meant by lifting up "holy" hands?

b. How does James show that it is incompatible to offer prayers one moment while arguing with, or cursing, our brethren the next? James 3:8-10 What was *his* conclusion about this? James 3:10b

c. Do you recognize that your prayers are hindered when you are at odds with others? Read 1 Peter 3:7 for an example of this in regard to husbands and wives. (You may also see Matthew 5:23-24.) Share your thoughts.

The conditions are laid down for the men—they are to pray in the assembly, lifting up holy hands, without wrath or doubting. Now Paul gives his word to the *women* who come to worship.

2. What does his command in verses 9-10 deal with?

   a. Why is this an important subject (in or out of the church)?

3. How, specifically, were they to adorn themselves? v. 9

   a. Describe what you think this means.

The word clothing (proper clothing—NASB) is the Greek word *katastole*, which encompasses not only the clothing itself, but the whole demeanor. Modesty (NASB) is *aidas*, which speaks of modesty with humility.

    b. Why is it *humble* to dress modestly?

Discreetly—*sophrosunes*—speaks of self-control, especially in regard to sexual behavior or passion.

    c. Why is it important for a woman, especially a Christian woman, to dress discreetly?

4. How were they *not* to adorn themselves? v. 9b

    a. Do you think Paul meant they were *never* to braid their hair or wear jewelry? What do you think he was trying to emphasize?

We would have to study the culture of this time to fully understand Paul's instruction here. Women in this culture often wore gold and jewelry woven into ornate hairdos to call attention to themselves and to display their wealth.

5. Rather than adorning herself with gold, jewelry, outlandish hairdos, and immodest clothing, with what should a Christian woman adorn herself? v. 10

   a. What do you think this means?

NASB says it best, "... By means of good works, as befits women making a claim to godliness."

6. *Something to think about:* Are you a woman making a claim to godliness? Are you in line with Paul's teaching on the subject of adornment? Share your thoughts on this subject.

This may seem like an insignificant thing, but if there is a check in your heart over something you have studied today—if the Lord has brought something to your mind—don't just shrug it off thinking that it's not a big deal or it really doesn't matter that much. If the Holy Spirit has brought it to your attention, then no matter how simple or even small, it is big enough for Him to care about. Submit to Him so that *your* prayers will not be hindered.

Review this week's memory verse.

Day 3
Read 1 Timothy 2:11-15

1. How did Paul command that a woman receive instruction in the church? v. 11

    a. Were the women allowed to *lead* the men? v.12 What, again, were they to do? (Take note of this idea, *to lead.*)

    b. *Digging Deeper:* See if you can share from the perspective of the world we live in today, what the emphasis is in this teaching of Paul. Do you think the culture and time we live in has any bearing on these words of Paul in this passage?

2. What is the order of authority as ordained by God through Paul in 1 Corinthians 11:3?

    a. Does your life submit to this order or do your actions and attitudes dispute it?

3. What historical fact does Paul point to as his evidence that man is to be in authority over woman? v. 13

a. How does he explain this in 1 Corinthians 11:8-9?

b. Looking back to the actual event in Genesis 2:18, what was God's design in creating the woman?

c. Read Genesis 2:21-24 for the remarkable details of the creation of woman. The man was created first and the woman was created to be his helper. Actually, she was created to be his other half. Another way of saying it would be she was his "completion." How does God see the man and woman who have joined together in the bond of marriage? (Genesis 2:24b)

Far from being a *lowly* position, we find equality as a person with differing roles and a God-given order of authority.

In verse 14, Paul brings into account the fact that it was Eve who was deceived in the garden. Eve was deceived; Adam sinned. Adam had been given the command (Genesis 2:16-17). Eve was tempted by Satan, succumbed to the temptation, and the Bible simply says "she gave also to her husband with her, and he ate" (Genesis 3:1-6). Adam should not have been following Eve's lead, Eve should have been submissive to Adam's authority, following *his* lead.

4. Of course, we know that the consequences of Adam and Eve's sin were so far reaching that they affected all of mankind. But, on a smaller level—on the level of a husband and a wife and a family—can you think of other consequences that follow when the woman is in authority over her husband, rather than being submissive to *His* authority? Take some time with this.

5. Paul makes an interesting statement in verse 15. Fill in the following spaces:

"Nevertheless she will be saved _____
if they continue in _____ with
_____" (NKJV).

It is likely that Paul is still considering the fall of Adam and Eve. We know that one of the effects of their sin was pain in childbirth, and yet there would be a continuation in this way of the life process.

This would actually be the woman's greatest contribution to the world; her greatest achievement; her crowning glory—especially as we consider the birth of the Christ child—but even as we consider the raising of godly children to carry on in the next generation.

   a. *If you are a mother*, have you recognized the great contribution you have to make to this world in the raising of godly children? If you haven't realized the importance of your role, how might this new perspective help you as you continue on in this difficult and demanding job?

In today's world, being a wife and mother gets little respect. But in God's eyes, it is the perfect fulfillment of His design for the woman (unless He has called you to a life of celibacy). Even if you are a woman who has never had children, being a support and helper to your husband is your way of achieving God's purpose for your life.

    b. How have you regarded your role as wife and/or mother up until now?

    c. Has God's word on this subject altered your perspective?

Review this week's memory verse.

Day 4

Overview of 1 Timothy 2

Today we will be looking at the passage we have studied this week as a whole. The goal is to find the main lessons the Lord has for us from this chapter. Don't worry about being clever or profound—just do your best!

Find the Facts ...
1. See if you can state the *content* of this week's passage in a couple of sentences. (Who is speaking, what is taking place, what is the main subject?)

Look for the Heart...

2. What do you think is the main *lesson* of this passage? (What spiritual truths are taught here? Is there a command to obey, a warning to heed, a promise to claim?)

Hear Him Speak...

3. Look for a *personal application* from the content of this passage. It should come from the lesson you got from the chapter (question 2). How will you apply the lesson to yourself?

4. Was there a particular verse that ministered to you this week? What was it and how did it minister to you?

5. Write out your memory verse *from memory*!

NOTES

1 TIMOTHY 3

Paul begins this portion of his letter to Timothy with words that are characteristic of the Pastoral Epistles and found only in them. *"This is a faithful saying"* signifies that the statement referred to is one upon which the believer can rest with confidence—the word faithful meaning *trustworthy*. On two occasions a fuller statement is given (1 Timothy 1:15 and 4:9)—*"This is a faithful saying and worthy of all acceptance."* Paul wants his readers to know that his statements are trustworthy and, therefore, to be fully accepted.

The theme of today's lesson will be spiritual leadership.

Day 1
Read 1 Timothy 3:1-7

1. What is the trustworthy statement Paul wants his readers to take to heart? v. 1

1st Timothy 3

The names bishop, pastor, and elder are all descriptions of the same person—the overseer of the local church. The word for bishop means *overseer*, elder means an *old man* (the elders were mature people with spiritual wisdom and experience), and pastor means *shepherd*.

   a. *Desires* (NKJV) is better translated *aspires* (NASB). How would you explain the idea of aspiring to something? (You may wish to look up the word *aspire* in your dictionary.)

The Greek word for aspire—*orego*—means to reach out after or to stretch out oneself to grasp something, but it does not convey the negative connotation of grasping.

   b. Explain why it would be a good thing to *aspire* to the position of pastor, but a bad thing to grasp or grapple for the office.

2. According to Paul's words in verse 1, what kind of a work is the office of pastor or bishop?

The Greek word for good is *kalos*, which is equivalent to the word *noble*.

a. How would you define the word noble? Do you see this as a noble work?

It is revealing that Paul does not proceed by telling us details about the work or office of the overseer but, instead, he lists the personal qualifications necessary for one to hold that office. Paul's emphasis is not on the character of the *office*, but on the character of the *man*, and he sets before us a standard of excellence.

3. In verse 2, Paul begins his list of qualifications for the pastorate with what is possibly the key to them all—that he is *blameless* or, another way of saying it would be, *above reproach*. Because we know that no one is *sinless*, what do you think these words indicate about the type of man who may hold the office of pastor?

   a. Beside each of the qualifications given in verse 2, write your best understanding of what this would mean.

   ⚜ *husband of one wife:*

   ⚜ *temperate:*

   ⚜ *sober-minded:*

✣ *of good behavior:*

✣ *hospitable:*

✣ *able to teach:*

4. Verse 3 gives a list of five negative traits (NKJV most clear.) What five things is this man *not* to be?

1.
2.
3.
4.
5.

   a. Take one of these negative character traits and share why it would be important for a pastor *not* to be given to such a thing.

   b. Among the five negative traits, verse 3 names one which is positive. What is it and why is it an important characteristic for a pastor?

5. Verses 4-7 give three more qualifications for the aspiring pastor, as well as the reason for each qualification. List each of the qualifications and the reasons for them.

verses 4-5
Qualification:

Paul's reasoning:

verse 6
Qualification:

Paul's reasoning:

verse 7
Qualification:

Paul's reasoning:

6. Look back over all the qualifications for pastor. Do these verses give you a new perspective of the character required, as well as the high calling of the office of pastor? Share your thoughts.

This week's memory verse: "To aspire to leadership is an honorable ambition." 1 Timothy 3:1 NEB

Day 2
Read 1 Timothy 3:8-13

Paul now moves to the qualifications for the office of deacon. In reading through these verses we notice quickly that the qualifications for deacon are quite similar and often the same as those for overseer. The position, however, is not the same. While the pastor "oversees" the church, ministering to the spiritual needs of the people, shepherding and teaching, the deacon (which means *servant*) sees to the more administrative details.

1. What are the first four qualifications Paul mentions in verse 8?

    a. Two qualities are added to Paul's previous list—*reverence* and *not double-tongued*. Explain your understanding of each of these.

2. Paul adds that the deacon must be *one who holds to the mystery of faith with a clear conscience*. Perhaps we could say this one *lives* by the principles that he claims to *believe*. Why is this important for the spiritual leader?

a. Can you think of a way in which a deacon could *first be proved* (verse 10), before being called in as deacon? (You may refer to verse 6 again.)

3. In what four ways are the wives of deacons to behave, according to verse 11?

1.
2.
3.
4.

a. Why would the behavior of deacons' wives be important?

It is sometimes felt that verse 11 refers not just to wives of deacons, but to women who serve in the role of deaconess (see Romans 16:1 for the example of Phoebe, servant—*diakonas*—of the church). We may apply these words to any woman who serves in a leadership position.

b. How important is the home life of the deacon (as with the pastor)? v. 12 Why do you think this is so?

4. What are two of the great benefits of *serving well as deacons*, according to verse 13?

a. Can you think of some other benefits of serving well in leadership positions in the church?

5. *Digging Deeper:* In Acts 6, we see what many believe to be the introduction of the position of deacon. Read Acts 6:1-7 and answer these questions:

   a. What was the situation that necessitated the selection of others to help?

   b. What were the qualifications of those who would be chosen?

   c. To what important work would the apostles be able to devote themselves as a result of the aid of these seven men?

   d. What seems to be the result of this further structuring of the early church?

We notice in Acts 6:6 that the seven chosen men were brought before the apostles, prayed for and hands were laid upon them. Though the position appeared of a practical nature, it required spiritual men with a spiritual calling.

6. If you are of the mind that "to aspire to leadership is an honorable ambition" and you have a strong desire to lead in some way, has what you have studied this far in 1 Timothy 3 given you perspective on the way to attain such a position? Share how you will prepare yourself to take a leadership position in your church, if the Lord thus calls.

Review this week's memory verse.

Day 3
Read 1 Timothy 3:14-16

Verse 15 gives us what is commonly believed to be the theme of Paul's first letter to Timothy. He says *"I write so that you may know how you ought to conduct yourself in the house of God."*

1. What three descriptive titles does Paul use for the church in verse 15?

The terms Paul uses are expressions of the holy character and solemn dignity of the church.

a. Do you understand why it was so important to Paul that Timothy teach the believers at Ephesus how to conduct themselves in the church?

2. In what way do you see the church as more than just a building (*house*) but actually a *household* (NASB)? You may see Ephesians 2:19-21 and 1 Peter 2:5.

   a. In simple terms, who makes up the church?

   b. To whom does it belong? Colossians 1:18a

3. Do you see God as the *living* God? Share your understanding of this fact and how you know it to be true.

   a. How do you see your church as the *church of the living God*?

Paul calls the church the pillar and ground (foundation or support) of the truth—giving us a picture of the body of Christ (you and I, as the church of the living God), being the foundation and pillar of all Divine revelation, including the gospel of Christ, upon which our faith is built. He moves on quickly in verse 16 to spell out for us the great mystery of godliness, which is the ministry of Jesus Christ.

It is commonly held that the six statements of Paul's proclamation were actually six lines of an early Christian hymn, revealing six truths about our Lord.

4. *Digging Deeper:* After each line of this hymn, briefly share the Scriptural teaching:

✤ *God was manifested in the flesh*—John 1:1, 14; Philippians 2:5-7

✤ *Justified in the Spirit*—Romans 1:4

✤ *Seen by angels*—(notice the progression from the announcement of His birth to his ascension) Luke 1:26-33; Matthew 1:18-21; Luke 2:6-14; Mark 1:13; Luke 22:39-43; Matthew 28:1-6; Acts 1:9-11

✤ *Preached among the Gentiles*—Matthew 28:19-20; Acts 1:8

✤ *Believed on in the world*—Acts 2:41

✤ *Received up in glory*—Acts 1: 9; Hebrews 1:3b; Philippians 2:9-11

5. What did Paul say was the one aim of his personal ministry? 1 Corinthians 2:2 (See also 1 Corinthians 1:23a)

   a. Why is the message of Jesus Christ the message of the church? See John 14:6 and John 8:32

Review this week's memory verse.

Day 4
Overview of 1 Timothy 3

Today we will be looking at the passage we have studied this week as a whole. The goal is to find the main lessons the Lord has for us from this chapter. Don't worry about being clever or profound—just do your best!

Find the Facts...
1. See if you can state the *content* of this week's passage in a couple of sentences. (Who is speaking, what is taking place, what is the main subject?)

Look for the Heart...

2. What do you think is the main *lesson* of this passage? (What spiritual truths are taught here? Is there a command to obey, a warning to heed, a promise to claim?)

Hear Him Speak...

3. Look for *a personal application* from the content of this passage. It should come from the lesson you got from the chapter (question 2). How will you apply the lesson to yourself?

4. Was there a particular verse that ministered to you this week? What was it and how did it minister to you?

5. Write out your memory verse *from memory*!

NOTES

1 TIMOTHY 4

In chapter 4, Paul turns his thoughts once again to the subject of the false teaching in Ephesus, clearing up some very specific problems, as well as giving a general warning to the church as to the very real dangers involved. Predominantly, though, this portion of Paul's letter is a personal exhortation to Timothy in his position as pastor and as a Christian. In his commentary on 1 Timothy, John MacArthur calls *his* chapters on 1 Timothy 4:6-16, "Qualities of an excellent minister." Warren Wiersbe entitles his chapter on this same portion of Scripture, "How to be a man of God." From either perspective, whether from the perspective of a spiritual leader, or simply a man (or woman) of God, these words will be invaluable to us.

Day 1
Read 1 Timothy 4:1-5

In verses 1 and 2, Paul clearly warns Timothy and the church of the already advancing problem of apostasy. The word apostasy means *a willful turning away from the truth of the Christian faith.*

1. According to these verses:

    a. When will this take place?

The latter times began with the resurrection of Christ and will continue until His return.

    b. By whose authority does Paul make this declaration?

    c. How does Paul describe what will take place?

In verse 2, Paul is obviously speaking of the false teachers—the *liars*—who will deceive some in the church to turn away from their faith.

This word was given by Paul to Timothy for the church at Ephesus, but it is every bit as important for us today—perhaps even more—as the second coming of Christ draws near, bringing with it an end to Satan's demonic reign. It is certain that as that time draws nearer, this opposition to the truth will grow stronger and this warning will be more needful than ever.

2. Jesus warned us about the "latter times" in Mark 13:21-23. What did He say?

    a. How do the words *"to deceive, if possible, even the elect"* strike you and help you to understand the dangers of false teaching for us today?

3. The antidote to *false teaching* is *truth*. Knowing the truth, believing the truth, practicing the truth, and living the truth. Who is the truth? John 14:6a

   a. How does Colossians 2:6-10 help you understand how to be established in the truth?

   b. Share some thoughts as to how you can equip yourself *not to be led astray*.

4. In verse 3, Paul names two clearly false teachings that were being taught at that time. What were they?

   a. Does God's word teach that marriage is forbidden? See Genesis 2:21-24 and Matthew 19:3-6.

   b. Does God's word teach that certain foods are to be rejected? See Genesis 1:29-31; Mark 7:15a; Acts 10:9-15; 1 Corinthians 10:25, 31

   c. What is Paul's stand on these things? 1 Timothy 4:4-5

The very word of God has confirmed to us that all that He made is good!

5. *Digging Deeper:* It is a distraction, at the very least, for believers to be kept focused on legalistic worldly matters rather than finding their salvation in Christ alone. Read the following two Colossian passages for Paul's words *against* such false teaching and *toward* the truth:

⚜ *Against false teaching:* Colossians 2:18-23

⚜ *Toward the truth:* Colossians 3:1-4

This week's memory verse: "Do you not know that those who run in a race all run, but only one receives the prize? Run in such a way that you may win." 1 Corinthians 9:24

Day 2
Read 1 Timothy 4:6-11

Paul knew Timothy's position to oversee the church at Ephesus, was difficult and demanding, and he knew that he would need personal direction and exhortation in order to fulfill that role. In chapter 3, we saw the *character* qualities necessary for one who would lead in the church. In the following verses (including our verses for tomorrow), Paul speaks directly to Timothy about his position, as well as his personal walk and growth. Verses 6-11 give us five necessities for the pastor, Timothy.

1. In what way, according to Paul, would Timothy prove to be a good minister of Jesus Christ? v. 6a

    a. What "things" would Paul have meant here? (See verses 1-5 again.)

    b. Is this still an important work for the pastor and others in leadership?

2. On what was Timothy himself to be nourished? v. 6

Timothy was to continue on in the manner he had begun—continuing in the doctrines he had been taught as a child, as well as those he had been taught by Paul. According to verse 6 NASB, he was to be "*constantly* nourished on the words of the faith."

    a. How can we be *constantly* nourished on the words of faith and good doctrine?

    b. How does Romans 6:16-18 help you see the importance of our obedience and commitment to sound teaching?

1st Timothy 4

    c. How does Jesus himself encourage us in the rewards of the constant nourishment of His word? John 8:31-32

3. In what manner was Timothy to treat "old wives' fables?" v. 7

    a. Paul spoke of these same distracting tales in 1 Timothy 1:4. What did he say was the problem with all that useless talk?

Timothy's job was to further the administration of God which is by faith (1 Timothy 1:4 NASB). Anything that did not have that aim and purpose was to be rejected.

    b. Are there any teachings or theories, worldly fables or myths that God has shown you to have nothing to do with? Why might that be?

4. Timothy was to:

- ✤ Verse 6a—Point out false teaching to the brethren.
- ✤ Verse 6b—Be constantly nourished on words of faith and good doctrine.
- ✤ Verse 7—Pay no attention to old wives' fables.
- ✤ Verse 7b—_____.

    a. What other type of exercise does Paul speak of here? v. 8a

    b. Is bodily exercise profitable? Contrast the profit of bodily exercise with godliness.

Exercise (discipline, NASB) is from *gumnazo*, from which we get the words gymnasium and gymnastics. It speaks of rigorous, strenuous training.

5. In verse 10, Paul uses two other words in describing our pursuit of godliness. What are they?

Verse 10 NASB says, *"For it is for this we labor and strive ..."*

Labor—*kopiao*—means to work to the point of weariness and exhaustion. Strive—*agonizomai*—is the source of our word agony and means to engage in a struggle.

    a. With these meanings in mind, describe how Paul intends for Timothy (and us) to pursue godliness.

    b. How have you found it to be hard work, and even a struggle, to live a godly life?

    c. Why are you willing to work so hard in order to pursue godliness? See verse 10, but share in your own words.

6. Timothy was not only to live out what Paul was commanding him, but he was to command (*prescribe*, NASB) and teach these things as well. In what way might encouraging another to discipline themselves to godliness be like a prescription?

   a. Are you disciplining yourself to godliness? Are you encouraging others to do the same?

Review this week's memory verse.

Day 3
Read 1 Timothy 4:12-16

In today's section, Paul gives five more words of exhortation.

1. Rather than being ashamed or handicapped by his age (Timothy was probably in his 30's at this time), Paul gave Timothy a way of compensation—*Let no one despise your youth, but* ... but what?

Timothy may have been comparatively young at that time to be in such a position of authority but in spiritual experience and growth he was mature.

   a. Consider what each of these aspects of Timothy's life refer to:

- word: *The way Timothy would talk.* (example)

- conduct:

- love:

- faith:

- purity:

   b. If all these aspects of Timothy's life proved him to be an example to the believers, why would his chronological age be of no detriment to his ministry?

Paul's words to Timothy are actually, "<u>Let</u> no one despise your youth ..." Evidently Paul saw this as a possible problem for Timothy. Is there anything that you have allowed to keep you from serving others or following God *confidently* into ministry? Perhaps you think you are too young, too old, too shy, or too fearful. Maybe you feel you haven't been educated enough or that you simply aren't smart enough or spiritual enough—Satan always points to that area in which we feel most inadequate. Perhaps we could take Paul's word to *us* to be, "Let no one look down on <u>you</u>, but rather, in word, in conduct, in love, in faith, in purity, show yourself an example to the believers!"

   c. Will you make an effort to live in such a godly way that you <u>can</u> minister to others in *spite* of your own personal weaknesses?

2. Paul's second word of exhortation gives Timothy specific direction for his public ministry. To what three things was he to give attention? v. 13

   a. Why is it important for the church to *hear* and not just to be told about God's Word?

   b. Look up the word exhortation and write its meaning here. Why do we need to be exhorted with God's Word?

   c. Timothy was also to teach God's Word ("give attention to ... *doctrine*"). Read Nehemiah 8:8 (NASB good) to get an understanding of what the teacher of God's Word does.

3. Of what was Timothy to take special care? v. 14a

John MacArthur says that Timothy's gift included evangelism, preaching, teaching, and leadership. We see that Timothy's *gift* was actually Timothy's *calling*.

4. Verse 15 is a call to Timothy to a total commitment to his work. How does Paul say he is to commit himself to *these things*?

Verse 15 says, "Take *pains* with these things; be absorbed in them." Oh, the amazing things God can do with those who consciously and willingly absorb themselves in the things that make them fit for His ministry!

    a. What will be the result of Timothy's total commitment to his ministry and calling? v. 15b

    b. What do you see as the benefit of the spiritual leader's progress being evident to his flock?

5. Paul tells Timothy that he is to pay close attention to two things—himself and his doctrine (his teaching). In what manner might he fulfill this word of Paul's exhortation:

✤ *for himself?*

✤ *for his teaching?*

    a. What would happen as Timothy continued in these things? v. 16b

6. See if you can take our memory verse and apply it to Paul's words of exhortation to Timothy in our passage today.

a. Are you running in such as way that *you* may win? Are there any changes that you might need to make? Are you willing to make them?

Review this week's memory verse.

Day 4
Overview of 1 Timothy 4

Today we will be looking at the passage we have studied this week as a whole. The goal is to find the main lessons the Lord has for us from this chapter. Don't worry about being clever or profound—just do your best!

Find the Facts ...
1. See if you can state the *content* of this week's passage in a couple of sentences. (Who is speaking, what is taking place, what is the main subject?)

Look for the Heart ...
2. What do you think is the main *lesson* of this passage? (What spiritual truths are taught here? Is there a command to obey, a warning to heed, a promise to claim?)

Hear Him Speak...

3. Look for a *personal application* from the content of this passage. It should come from the lesson you got from the chapter (question 2). How will you apply the lesson to yourself?

4. Was there a particular verse that ministered to you this week? What was it and how did it minister to you?

5. Write out your memory verse *from memory*!

NOTES

1 TIMOTHY 5

In chapter 5, Paul begins by giving Timothy a picture of the church that will help him in dealing with the people of his congregation. The picture is that of a family—the church being like a family and Timothy, as pastor, relating to and caring for those in his congregation as he would his own. Paul specifically speaks of the obligation of Timothy and the church to two groups of people—widows and elders.

Day 1
Read 1 Timothy 5:1-8

Paul begins by laying the foundation for Timothy's relationship with and approach to the various people in his congregation. The immediate perspective seems to deal with confrontation of sin.

1. In confronting the sin or error of an older man in his church, how is Timothy *not* to confront him?

    a. What should he do instead?

The word rebuke—*epiplesso*—refers to a harsh or violent rebuke. Appeal—*parakaleo*—can mean to encourage, admonish, or entreat, but the best translation is to strengthen, or to come alongside and hold up the one who is weak.

    b. Why should *encouragement* be used, rather than rebuke, in the case of confronting one who is in error?

    c. How can this confrontation actually be seen as *coming alongside* and *strengthening* the erring one?

2. Paul says the older man is to be appealed to as a father. How is Timothy to appeal to:

The younger men?
The older women?
The younger women?

    a. What additional word is given in regard to Timothy's treatment of the younger women? (v. 2) Why would this be important?

Paul now turns his attention to the subject of widows.

3. How does Paul say we, as the church, are to regard widows? v. 3

This word honor encompasses the meanings of *showing respect or care, treating graciously, supporting.* From the context of this passage, we see that honoring the widow would be to provide for her basic needs, but we also see that there are certain qualifications for being considered a *widow indeed*.

4. According to verse 4, who would be first to provide for the needy widow?

   a. What two things would the child or grandchild learn in providing for the needs of the widowed relative?

   b. Share any thoughts you may have on the benefit of a child or grandchild *making some return to their parents.*

   c. What was Paul's pronouncement on the one who wouldn't care for his needy relative? v. 8

5. Verses 5 gives a description (or we might actually call it a definition) of the widow who Paul labels a "widow indeed." What three things does he tell us about her?

6. Luke 2:36-37 gives us an example of just such a godly widow. Read these verses about Anna and make note of what you learn of her.

a. For an added blessing, scan verses 21-38 of Luke 2 and see if you can determine the special way in which God showed honor to this widow who dedicated her life to Him.

This week's memory verse: "You shall rise up before the grayheaded and honor the aged, and you shall revere your God; I am the Lord." Leviticus 19:32

Day 2
Read 1 Timothy 5:9-16

In the first day of our lesson, we considered the financial support of widows. Today we will look at widows from the perspective of their qualification for ministry in the church.

1. See Titus 2:3-5. This passage gives us a basic understanding of the part these women would have in the ministry. From verses 4-5:

   a. Who were they to teach?

   b. What were they to teach them?

   1.
   2.
   3.
   4.
   5.
   6.
   7.

c. Do you see the need for this type of teaching today? If you are *younger*—are you willing to be taught in this way? If you are *older*—do you see the need to be this type of teacher? Share your thoughts.

2. In 1 Timothy 5, Paul refers to a list on which the widow's name would be placed, if she qualified for such ministry in the church. He gives three requirements for qualification:

1—verse 9a
2—verse 9b
3—verse 10a

a. Verse 10 continues by defining the types of good works for which this woman would be known. List them here:

1.
2.
3.
4.
5.

3. Do you know any widows like those we are learning about today? Do you realize the valuable asset they might prove to be in your life? Looking over the requirements for their service, what do you see that you might be able to glean from their lives?

4. Who was not to be placed on the list? v. 11a

    a. Paul gives two reasons for the younger widow not to be on the list of ministering widows, what are they:

    1—*verses 11-12?*

Paul is not criticizing these young widows for *desiring* to remarry; he is simply predicting that this will be the common occurrence. It seems that in being placed on the list of ministering widows there was a pledge taken—a commitment made to the Lord to serve Him in this manner.

    2—*verse 13?*

Paul also sees that the younger widows are not mature enough to commit to such a ministry at this point in their lives. In fact, from the passage in Titus, we see that they are the *very ones* to whom the older women are to minister.

5. What was Paul's counsel to the younger widow? v. 14

    a. In what way do you see Paul's counsel to get married, bear children and keep house to be the very thing needed to curtail the activity mentioned in verse 13?

Paul finishes his thoughts back where he began—now speaking specifically to women—if you have a relative who is a widow, then you must provide for her needs, so that the church may help those who are "widows indeed."

Review this week's memory verse.

Day 3
Read 1 Timothy 5:17-25

Paul now returns to the subject of elders. In chapter 3, we learned of their qualifications for ministry; in chapter 4, Timothy was given personal exhortation in his position as pastor; and in this chapter we will discuss the duties of the church *to* the pastor/elder.

1. What is the elder who rules well worthy of? v. 17

We have already seen that the word honor speaks of *showing respect* and *treating graciously.* All elders would be worthy of honor, but in this passage Paul speaks of a *double honor.*

   a. Three duties of this worthy elder are mentioned in verse 17:

   1.
   2.
   3.

2. How, or in what manner, will this elder rule, according to verse 17?

The adverb *well* in "rule well" is *kalos*, which could be translated "with excellence." The elder worthy of double honor will rule in a way that is above the ordinary—he won't just rule, he will rule with *excellence*.

    a. How will he work at his preaching and teaching?

Labor (work hard, NASB) is from *kopiao*, meaning to work to the point of exhaustion.

    b. Do you imagine that all pastors rule well and work at their preaching to the point of exhaustion? Is it clear why the man who does so should be worthy of double honor?

    c. How does 1 Thessalonians 5:12-13 encourage *you* to give double honor to those who minister faithfully to you?

We know that this word honor also speaks of *support*.

3. What instruction does verse 18 give on this point? (See if you can explain what it means not to *muzzle the ox while he is threshing*.)

It's interesting that Paul has taken both from the Old and the New Testaments in this verse—quoting first from the words of Moses and then confirming them with the words of Jesus Himself.

a. Why is it important that those who oversee the church are compensated for their work? (You may see verse 17 again for insight.)

4. Paul is careful to protect elders from false accusations. What would be the *only way* that Timothy should receive an accusation against an elder according to verse 19?

   a. What was Timothy to do if there *were* two or three witnesses to the wrongdoing of the elder? v. 20

   b. Paul realized that Timothy might possibly be swayed by his own feelings toward the elder. How did Paul ensure that this would not be a problem? v. 21

The subject of the sin of an elder brings Paul back to the point of the original calling and ordination.

5. What was one of the original restrictions Paul made in listing the qualifications for elders? 1 Timothy 3:6

Verse 22 agrees with this fact—"Do not lay hands upon anyone [for ordination] too hastily."

1st Timothy 5

a. Why would *Timothy* be responsible for the sin of an elder too hastily ordained?

b. How would *time* be the greatest factor in helping Timothy to know the quality of person he was ordaining? vv. 24-25

Have you ever thought about the fact that whether your sins go before you or follow after you, they are eventually evident (verse 25 says that deeds which are other than good cannot be concealed)? We all know that no one is perfect—but we must never use this as an excuse to sin. These verses are not speaking of imperfection, but sin.

In the same manner, it is a wonderful thing to know that whether you realize it or not, *"deeds that are good are quite evident!"* As you live your life each day you make choices. The choices you make not only make up who you are becoming but can also open or shut doors for your further usefulness in the ministry of the Lord. Make your choices wisely so that you may be one who can be called upon to minister in the church.

6. Meditate on 2 Timothy 2:20-21 for a few moments and share anything the Lord may reveal to you about the vessel He is in the process of making *you*.

Review this week's memory verse.

Day 4
Overview of 1 Timothy 5

Today we will be looking at the passage we have studied this week as a whole. The goal is to find the main lessons the Lord has for us from this chapter. Don't worry about being clever or profound—just do your best!

Find the Facts ...

1. See if you can state the *content* of this week's passage in a couple of sentences. (Who is speaking, what is taking place, what is the main subject?)

Look for the Heart ...

2. What do you think is the main *lesson* of this passage? (What spiritual truths are taught here? Is there a command to obey, a warning to heed, a promise to claim?)

Hear Him Speak ...

3. Look for a *personal application* from the content of this passage. It should come from the lesson you got from the chapter (question 2). How will you apply the lesson to yourself?

4. Was there a particular verse that ministered to you this week? What was it and how did it minister to you?

5. Write out your memory verse *from memory*!

NOTES

1 TIMOTHY 6

As we consider the final chapter of Paul's first letter to Timothy, we see him continue to give Timothy instruction concerning specific groups of people--slaves, false teachers, the rich--concerning the issue of money, as well as some final words of exhortation for Timothy himself.

Day 1
Read 1 Timothy 6:1-5

Paul begins this chapter with words to believing slaves concerning their slave/master relationship. We might think of the employee/employer relationship as we consider these words.

1. In what manner is the Christian slave to regard his unbelieving master according to verse 1?

   a. Why is it important that he do so?

b. If you work for a non-Christian, do you consider it your duty as a Christian to show him respect as your employer? Do you recognize that your attitude as an employee is connected to your Christian witness?

2. Why might it be that a Christian slave would have a different (or less respectful) attitude toward a Christian master than he would if that master was an unbeliever? v. 2 (You may see Galatians 3:28 for help.)

a. How does Paul say the believing slave ought to serve the believing master and why?

Paul's aim is always to the highest: "... let them serve them *all the more* ..." Here we can ask ourselves the question, "Have I ever taken advantage of my employer (or any superior in the workplace) due to the fact that he is a brother (or she is a sister) in Christ?"

3. Look up the following verses and share the point that stands out to you about the standard to which you are called to live in your dealings with *your* employer:

✣ Ephesians 6:5-6; Colossians 3:22

✣ Ephesians 6:7-8; Colossians 3:23-24

✣ Titus 2:9-10

✣ 1 Peter 2:18

   a. If you are in a difficult work situation or even personal situation (with your husband or parents), is there a verse in this list which helps you get perspective on how God desires you to conduct yourself? How will you apply this verse?

Now Paul picks up the thread, once again, of false teachers and their teaching.

4. In verse 3, Paul points out three signs of false teaching. List them here.

   a. Using this as a description of false teaching, see if you can explain how to tell when you are receiving true *godly* teaching.

5. How does Paul describe the false teacher in verse 4a?

1.
2.
3.

   a. What are some of the negative *results* of those things in which they interest themselves? vv. 4b-5a

   b. How does verse 5 describe their spiritual condition?

   c. What does Paul see as the motivation of their heart? v. 5b

6. James 3:13-18 gives us a definition of *true* wisdom. From these verses, how do we recognize one who is truly wise? (v. 13)

   a. What are the characteristics of true wisdom? (v. 17)

   b. What will be the fruit of the *"seed sown in peace by those who make peace?"* (v. 18)

This week's memory verse: "But godliness with contentment is great gain." 1 Timothy 6:6 NKJV

Day 2
Read 1 Timothy 6:6-10

Paul finished his description of false teachers by revealing the motivation of their teaching to be a financial one, saying that they "... *suppose that godliness is a means of gain.*"

1. According to verse 6, *is* godliness a means of gain? What is the qualifying factor? Do you think this verse is speaking of financial gain?

Godliness—*eusebeia*—means piety, reverence, or likeness to God. It describes holiness, spirituality, and virtue. Contentment—*autarkeia*—means self-sufficiency and speaks of being satisfied and sufficient. In the world one might find contentment in his ability to provide for himself (self-sufficiency), but as Christians, we find our sufficiency in Christ.

2. How does Paul describe this sense of sufficiency in Christ in 2 Corinthians 3:5?

    a. What did he say about himself in regard to contentment? Philippians 4:11

    b. How did he describe what he had learned, in Philippians 4:12?

c. What foundational belief did Paul have which gave him the ability to be content in any situation? Philippians 4:13 (Do you have this foundational belief?)

3. Why is it that we should be content with what we have been given by God, according to 1 Timothy 6:7?

   a. With what two main provisions of God should we be able to be content? v. 8

   b. Are you content with these basic provisions? Consider what you might be willing to do to make certain that you have more.

4. What does Paul say happens to the one who desires to get rich? v. 9

   a. Have you ever been, or are you now, snared by the desire to be rich or to have much in the way of possessions? How was your walk with the Lord at that time?

5. What does Paul say about the love of money? v. 10a

a. If a person is pursuing money and things, how does that hamper their pursuit of God? See Matthew 6:24

b. What is likely to happen to them according to verse 1 Timothy 6:10?

c. What wise words do you find tucked away in Proverbs 23:4 which you can apply to yourself when trapped in the pursuit of riches?

6. *Digging Deeper:* Read the words of Jesus in Matthew 6:31-33. Make note of the clear perspective Matthew 6:33 gives us on: 1) What we, as Christians, are to pursue; 2) What we will gain *when* we are pursuing these things.

Review this week's memory verse.

Day 3
Read 1 Timothy 6:11-21

1. In verse 11, Paul addresses Timothy as a man of God. What does he exhort this man of God to do? (v. 11a) What things?

Paul doesn't want Timothy to have a passive distrust of the pursuit of riches and the love of money, he wants him to *flee* from these things. The present tense of the verb "flee" indicates that it is to be a constant state for him—*constantly flee from these things.*

Oswald Chambers says of the cares of this world, the deceitfulness of riches, and the lust for other things, "We are never free from the recurring tides of this encroachment." In other words, fleeing from the pursuit of riches (etc.) is not something that we do once and for all—it is an attitude that we must maintain.

   a. Does your own experience agree with this idea? Share your thoughts on this subject.

2. If *fleeing* is running away from something—how would you define *pursuing*?

   a. What does Paul encourage Timothy to pursue? v. 11

b. Do you see yourself as being in pursuit of these virtues? How are you going about this?

Next, Paul exhorts Timothy to fight the good fight of faith, to take hold of the eternal life to which he was called, and, in verses 13-14, to keep the commandment (the entire revealed word of God which Timothy was called to preach) without stain or reproach.

3. How does Paul exhort us to "work out" our salvation in Philippians 2:12? How do these words fit in with Paul's charge to Timothy to *fight,* to *take hold*, and to *keep* the commandment?

   a. How did Paul testify of himself that this was the manner in which he "worked out" his salvation? 2 Timothy 4:7 (At the end of your life, are these words which you plan to be able to say?)

4. What instruction is Timothy to give those who are rich? v. 17a

   a. Who do they to fix their hope on, and why? v. 17b

Do you realize that God is the source of *all* good things that come your way? Notice the words of the psalmist who sees *God* as the source of his joy: *"All my springs of joy are in you"* (Psalm 87:7b NASB). Can you say this today?

5. The rich are instructed neither to be haughty nor to trust in uncertain riches—what *are* they to do? v. 18

Being will always lead to *doing*. Timothy, and all who read this letter, are encouraged to pursue righteousness, godliness, faith, love, perseverance, and gentleness. From the overflow of this kind of heart, good works will naturally follow.

   a. What will be the result of doing such good works? v. 19a How is this in keeping with Jesus' exhortation in Matthew 6:20a?

   b. Paul says that in doing these things, they will take hold of that which is life indeed. See if you can contrast the life that will be gained by those who pursue riches and the love of money with the life that will be gained by those who pursue godliness and good works. Which of these would you call *life indeed?*

6. One final word of exhortation is given in verses 20-21. What is it?

1st Timothy 6

It's interesting to take a look at the *verbs* that Paul uses in his final words in this letter to Timothy, they are—*flee* (from the love of money), *pursue* (godly virtues), *fight* (the good fight of faith), *take hold* (of your eternal life), *keep* (the commandment), and *guard* (what has been entrusted to you)—all strong words commanding action on the part of Timothy.

    a. Look at each of the following points and share on the one (or more) that you need to take to heart today, as you *work out your own salvation with fear and trembling.* What action do you need to take in order to:

✤ *Flee from the love of money?*

✤ *Pursue godly virtues?*

✤ *Fight the good fight of faith?*

✤ *Take hold of your eternal life?*

✤ *Keep the commandment?*

✤ *Guard what has been entrusted to you?*

Review this week's memory verse.

Day 4
Overview of 1 Timothy 6

Today we will be looking at the passage we have studied this week as a whole. The goal is to find the main lessons the Lord has for us from this chapter. Don't worry about being clever or profound—just do your best!

Find the Facts...

1. See if you can state the *content* of this week's passage in a couple of sentences. (Who is speaking, what is taking place, what is the main subject?)

Look for the Heart...

2. What do you think is the main *lesson* of this passage? (What spiritual truths are taught here? Is there a command to obey, a warning to heed, a promise to claim?)

Hear Him Speak...

3. Look for a *personal application* from the content of this passage. It should come from the lesson you got from the chapter (question 2). How will you apply the lesson to yourself?

4. Was there a particular verse that ministered to you this week? What was it and how did it minister to you?

5. Write out your memory verse *from memory*!

NOTES

2 TIMOTHY 1

As we begin to study the second letter of Paul to his "beloved son" Timothy, it would be helpful for us to get a pulse on the heart of its author. It is interesting that, as we study letters written *to* Timothy and perhaps think in the study of them that we will be learning *about* Timothy, we find even more that we have been given a glimpse into the heart, thoughts, priorities, attitudes, and desires of Paul, the writer. This particular letter will be no exception, as it is perhaps Paul's most personal letter—written shortly before his death from a cold, dark, and dirty prison cell at, undoubtedly, the loneliest time of his life. This story will unfold as we begin, verse by verse, to study his final letter, written in approximately 66 AD from prison in Rome (his second and final imprisonment) to the young pastor at Ephesus, Timothy. Paul is, in essence, passing the torch: handing the keys of the kingdom to the next generation of leaders, among whom Timothy is foremost.

What would you write to your loved ones if you knew you were at death's door? Would you let them know how dear they are to your heart and tell them of your love?

Would you encourage them in their faith, building them up in their strengths and admonishing them in their weaknesses? Would you leave them with a charge to fulfill their ministry and serve the Lord courageously? And would you, perhaps, share with them your own personal memories and sense of accomplishments in this life? Paul did all this and more in his final words to Timothy.

Day 1
Read 2 Timothy 1:1-5

1. By what title does Paul present himself in this, his second letter to Timothy?

    a. By whose will?

Paul sees his apostleship as a divine appointment. He was confident at this difficult point in his life that he stood strong in the will of God. Do you see yourself as being in God's will today?

    b. According to what promise?

The words *in Christ* are significant to the apostle Paul, who uses them almost as a statement of his belief system. Are you *in Christ* today? If so, then He is *in you*! Your life is identified with His and you can trust in His purpose, plan, and will for you—you are His!

    c. In what manner did Paul address Timothy? v. 2

    d. With what three words of godly encouragement did he open this letter to Timothy? v. 2

It seems that the words grace and peace are words in which Paul begins all of his letters. Only to Timothy does he include the word *mercy*: an encouragement to Timothy of God's tender loving-kindness toward him.

2. From verses 3-4, who is Paul thank*ful to?* Who is he thankful *for?*

Very typical in all of Paul's letters is an opening word of thanksgiving. Today's passage of Scripture as a whole actually sets the stage for what Paul plans to impart to Timothy throughout the rest of the letter.

3. Paul speaks of his service to God in these verses as a *present* activity, and yet we know that Paul was locked in a dark and filthy prison. See if you can determine some of the different ways Paul was actively serving God.

    a. Perhaps you are in some sort of prison in your life today. Look at 1 Thessalonians 5:16-22, and share some ways you can serve God no matter where you are or what your circumstances or *prison* may be. Might some of these very things depict Paul's service to God in the Roman prison?

4. How did Paul say he served God? v. 3 Look at the following words of Paul's personal testimony and share what he says:

✟ Acts 23:1

✟ Acts 24:16

✟ 2 Corinthians 1:12

   a. Do you think that having a clear conscience means that a person is *perfect*? What do you think it means?

   b. How can a person maintain a clear conscience? Are you careful to do this?

Note: Remember the words of 1 Timothy 4:2, when Paul spoke of a *seared* conscience. It is an extremely dangerous thing to allow your conscience to become hardened or numb so that you are no longer tenderhearted and open to God's voice. Conversely, if you are someone with a sensitive conscience—be thankful! Even though at times it may be uncomfortable, how much better for you to be quickly convicted so that you might be quickly restored.

5. How did Paul *remember* Timothy? v. 3 (Notice how this fulfills Paul's own words in 1 Thessalonians 5:17.)

   a. What was Paul's heart's desire? v. 4

6. What precious quality did Paul say he recognized in Timothy? v. 5

   a. How did Timothy come by this godly quality?

The word genuine means *sincere, unhypocritical, without pretense or deceit.*

   b. Using this definition, describe the faith of Timothy.

   c. How would you describe an insincere faith?

   d. Do you see yourself as having a sincere faith? Are you passing your faith on to the younger generation?

Lois and Eunice may have had no claims to fame during their lifetimes. They may have held no important positions, written no bestsellers, and been unrecognizable to anyone beyond their family and friends, and yet, the word of God holds them in honor. To the world, what they accomplished means little or nothing but to *God,* they accomplished a great work, imparting to young Timothy a sincere, transparent love of God and belief in His Son Jesus Christ.

This week's memory verse: "For God has not given us a spirit of timidity, but of power and love and discipline." 2 Timothy 1:7

Day 2
Read 2 Timothy 1:6-7

After opening his letter with words that were both loving and affirming, in verse 6 Paul begins his instruction to Timothy. It is said that this final letter to Timothy includes many admonitions with approximately twenty-five commands. Here is where we see Paul's authority as apostle surface. Although he is a beloved friend, he is also the figure of spiritual authority in Timothy's life and therefore in the position to pass along instructions, as from the Lord Himself.

1. Verse 6 follows the thoughts of verse 5, which speaks of Timothy's genuine faith. Because of Timothy's sincere faith, what did Paul remind him to do?

    a. Why was it that he could do this? v. 7

2. Looking again to 1 Thessalonians 5:19, what does Paul exhort the Thessalonians *not* to do?

The word quench means *to put out, or extinguish as a fire*. The Holy Spirit is often spoken of in Scripture as fire (see Matthew 3:11; Acts 2:3-4). We might think to ourselves, "I am too afraid to use my gifts—so I won't;" or, "I may make a mistake, or fail, or bring disgrace to God, etc."

a. Since it is the Holy Spirit who gives gifts (they are the gifts *of* the Holy Spirit), how might succumbing to our own fears or worries and not using our spiritual gifts be like quenching the Holy Spirit?

b. What does 1 Peter 4:10-11 have to say to us about this?

Paul is very clear to Timothy that, although he may be fearful (timid, NASB), this fear was *not* from God. The word for fear or timid in this passage (used only here in the New Testament) has a completely negative meaning. It speaks of cowardly, shameful fear, generated by a weak, selfish character. We know that Timothy had a genuine faith, but it may be just as true that Timothy was prone to cowardice and weakness (perhaps some of us can identify with him!).

3. If *God* did not give Timothy a spirit of fear, from whom would this spirit come?

a. When *you* are afraid of serving God (because of the possibility of personal failure), to whose voice are you listening—the voice of God, according to the teaching of His word—or the voice of His enemy (the one who comes only to rob, steal, and destroy)? What does Romans 8:15 have to say to us?

4. What kind of spirit does Paul say that God gives? (v. 7)

   a. Why would God give those who serve Him in this world a spirit of power? Whose power is this? Acts 1:8

   b. Why would God give those who serve Him a spirit of love? Where do we get this love? Romans 5:5

Sophronismos—discipline (NASB)—speaks of a sound and secure mind, and it also has the meaning of a self-controlled, disciplined, and prioritized mind. Verse 7 in the Amplified Bible says this: *"For God did not give us a spirit of timidity (of cowardice, of craven and cringing and fawning fear), but [He has given us a spirit] of power and of love and of calm and well-balanced mind and discipline and self-control."*

   c. Why would it be important for God's servant to have a spirit of discipline (NKJV: a sound mind)?

Do you find yourself lacking in any of these areas today? This passage says God has given us these things, therefore they are ours. Pray and ask God to manifest these qualities in your life, and be sure you let Him do so by stepping forward in expectation, believing Him to supply you with His power, His love, and His discipline when, and as, you need them.

Review this week's memory verse.

Day 3
Read 2 Timothy 1:8-18

Paul's second word of admonition, and the key thought of this chapter, is the call to Timothy *not to be ashamed*.

1. Of what two things did Paul exhort Timothy not to be ashamed? v. 8

    a. Rather than being ashamed, what did Paul encourage Timothy to do?

2. There is no one in this world that actually *wants* to suffer. But as Christians we learn that suffering is promised and it is also a privilege. What do the following verses say about suffering?

✣ Romans 8:16, 17

✣ 2 Timothy 2:3

✣ 2 Timothy 3:12

    a. Who is our example in suffering? 1 Peter 2:21

b. What should be our outlook when we suffer for righteousness sake? 1 Peter 4:13

c. What was Paul's greatest desire? Philippians 3:10

Paul didn't ask Timothy to join him in suffering for his mistakes or for sinfulness, but for *the gospel according to the power of God.* At the end of these words, Paul's thoughts naturally flow onward to the glorious working of God through Jesus Christ, our Savior.

3. According to verse 9a, what two things has God done for us?

   a. Were we called because we were good or had done something to earn his favor?

   b. When does this verse say this grace of God was granted to us?

There is much security in the words of verse 9. If you are insecure in your salvation, meditate on this verse and allow it to penetrate your heart and mind—this word is *God's truth!*

4. In His first appearing—the Incarnation—what two things did Jesus accomplish?

a. What is the gospel message? See 1 Corinthians 15:3-5

b. *Digging Deeper:* See 1 Corinthians 15:51-57 for a preview of the Christian's promise of life, immortality, and victory over death, as a result of the ministry of Jesus Christ. These words should excite you and bring you great hope!!!

It was this very message that Paul says he was appointed to preach. Can you think of a more exciting ministry than preaching this great news?! Paul says in verse 12, *"For this reason I also suffer these things ..."* Paul is speaking of his current imprisonment and impending death. His present suffering was because he was appointed a preacher and an apostle and a teacher of the gospel of Jesus Christ.

5. Was Paul ashamed of his chains? v.12 Why?

   a. What had Paul entrusted to Jesus Christ? (Your thoughts.)

6. What final two words of admonition did Paul give Timothy in chapter 1, which are reminiscent of words he wrote in 1 Timothy:

verse 13

verse 14

Both of these verses speak of God's Truth, which He has imparted to us by way of the Holy Scriptures.

    a. Have you allowed God's Word to be your standard—in other words, that which you use as the *guideline* for your life and behavior? If you are living by any other standard than by the Word of God, then you will never live the abundant life that God has planned for you. See Romans 12: 2 and share your thoughts.

    b. How does 2 Timothy 3:16-17 help you to realize the great usefulness of God's inspired word? Will you allow it to accomplish God's work in you?

"So keep my words in your mind as the pattern of sound teaching, given to you in the faith and love of Christ Jesus. Take the greatest care of the treasures which were entrusted to you by the Holy Spirit who lives within us." 2 Timothy 1:13-14 (Phillips)

Review this week's memory verse.

Day 4
Overview of 2 Timothy 1

Today we will be looking at the passage we have studied this week as a whole. The goal is to find the main lessons the Lord has for us from this chapter. Don't worry about being clever or profound—just do your best!

Find the Facts ...

1. See if you can state the *content* of this week's passage in a couple of sentences. (Who is speaking, what is taking place, what is the main subject?)

Look for the Heart ...

2. What do you think is the main *lesson* of this passage? (What spiritual truths are taught here? Is there a command to obey, a warning to heed, a promise to claim?)

Hear Him Speak ...

3. Look for a *personal application* from the content of this passage. It should come from the lesson you got from the chapter (question 2). How will you apply the lesson to yourself?

4. Was there a particular verse that ministered to you this week? What was it and how did it minister to you?

5. Write out your memory verse *from memory*!

NOTES

2 TIMOTHY 2

Paul begins this chapter with the words, *"You therefore, my son ..."* The word *therefore* connects the thoughts that will follow with what has been previously said. What *has* been previously said? Paul has reminded Timothy that he has been given a spirit of power and of love and of a sound mind from God ... therefore, he can be strong. Is this not true of us as well? Are we acting on this truth? How is God's Word making a difference in the way we live?

Day 1
Read 2 Timothy 2:1-7

1. Is Timothy to be strong in his own human strength, abilities, and talents or in any way in himself? In what is Timothy to be strong?

    a. How does 2 Corinthians 3:4-5 help us to see that in spiritual matters *our* strength is not enough? Where *do* we put our confidence?

b. How does Ephesians 6:10 help to point us in the right direction?

2. From what we have learned about Timothy so far, why is it important that Paul point him to *Christ* to find strength for his Christian walk and, even more, for his Christian service?

   a. If you are a person who is naturally timid, like Timothy, does it encourage you that you need not look to yourself or your own resources in your spiritual service, but that you will find your strength in God? See the encouraging words of 2 Corinthians 4:7.

3. Verse 2 gives Timothy perfect plan of discipleship. Look carefully at this verse and share the plan, with yourself in mind.

   a. Are you passing on those things that you are learning in church, at Bible study, and from the Lord in your devotion time? Think of an example of a time recently when you passed along some word of truth that you received.

It is said that we retain more of what we learn by passing the information along to others than in any other way.

We gain by *hearing* (listening to a message), we gain more by *seeing* (taking notes), even more by *discussing* what we've heard (going over our lessons with our group), and we gain the most from what we have heard by *passing it along to others* (teaching). Make this your practice!

Paul now gives Timothy three illustrations of the characteristics of a strong spiritual life—the *soldier*, the *athlete*, and the *farmer*.

4. Timothy is called to be a good soldier of Christ Jesus. What will Timothy be willing to do to be a good soldier? v. 3 Who is his example in *this* verse?

    a. What will the good soldier be careful *not* to do? v. 4 What do you think this means? (Spend a moment thinking about this.)

    b. If you think about the word entangle meaning, *being all tangled up in something*, why would it be important for a soldier to be *disengaged* from the affairs of this life? Why would this be important for the Christian minister?

Hebrews 12:1 (NASB) tells us to "*lay aside every encumbrance*, and the sin which so easily entangles us, and let us *run with endurance the race that is set before us.*"

2nd Timothy 2

    c. Are you a little too entangled in the affairs of this world? Do the things which belong to this world: the striving for money, success, things, the worries of clothing and style, gossip and intrigue, take a little too much of your thoughts, efforts, and time? What encumbrance might you need to *lay aside* in order to run with endurance the race that is set before *you*?

Verse 4 ends with the words, *"That he may please him who enlisted him as a soldier."* We know that it was Timothy's greatest desire to please his commander-in-chief, Jesus Christ. If this is your greatest desire, then you will have no problem laying aside those things that are of no eternal value, which have the ability to keep you distracted in your service.

5. What lesson does Paul teach Timothy through the example of the athlete? v. 5 What does this mean to you in your effort to serve Christ?

Speaking of the athlete's competition in the games, Paul says in 1 Corinthians 9:25, *"Now they do it to obtain a perishable crown, but we for an imperishable crown."*

    a. Paul was extremely careful to obey the rules (you may see 1 Corinthians 9:26-27). At the imminent close of his life, what sure hope does he express? 2 Timothy 4:8

6. In his example of the farmer, how does Paul describe the farmer? v. 6

We remember from a previous lesson that this word *hard-working* means to toil intensely, to sweat and strain to the point of exhaustion, if necessary. This is the emphasis of this verse—the diligent labor of this one who will receive a share of the crops.

   a. How might a pastor/teacher be compared to a farmer? What will be the results of his diligent toil?

The emphasis in all of these illustrations is the labor, diligence, and discipline necessary for success. Timothy must know that this will be his portion. Those of us who desire to serve the Lord must realize this as well. Consider what Paul says, for the Lord will "give you understanding in all things" (verse 7).

This week's memory verse: "… A vessel for honor, sanctified, useful to the Master, prepared for every good work." 2 Timothy 2:21b

Day 2
Read 2 Timothy 2:8-19

Paul's words to Timothy are, *"Remember Jesus Christ …"* (verse 8, NASB). One commentator says that these words should be spoken in the same manner as, "Remember the Alamo!" Paul is saying, *"Remember Jesus Christ, Timothy!"* He is your source, your strength, and your motivation for continuing on in the faith as a diligent, dedicated, and, if necessary, suffering servant.

2nd Timothy 2

1. As Paul exhorts Timothy to remember Jesus Christ, he points out two aspects of Christ's testimony. What are they? v. 8

    a. What does the fact that Jesus was raised from the dead reveal about who He is? You may see Acts 2:24.

    b. Think about the words *seed of David*. They speak of Jesus' earthly connection, showing his family heritage. What do they prove about Him?

Philippians 2:5-8 tells us that Jesus Christ, who existed in the form of *God*, emptied Himself, taking the form of a bond-servant, and being found in the appearance as a *man*, humbled Himself by becoming obedient to the point of death, even death on a cross. This was to be Timothy's example in service. This is to be our example in service. And this was Paul's example in service, as well as the very message that he was constrained to preach.

2. What did Paul say about his calling to preach the gospel message? 1 Corinthians 9:16

    a. How was his *present* suffering a result of this constraint? vv. 8-9

b. Why was he most willing to endure the consequences of fulfilling this, his ministry? v. 10

c. How does Romans 1:16 sum up Paul's respect for his message?

It was Paul's *ministry* to preach the message; it was Paul's *life* to follow the man. This was what he wanted Timothy to grasp. On that path there not only *might* be suffering, there surely would be. But remember, *Christ is our example* (1 Peter 2:21).

It is such a blessing to study the works of Paul, as he often stops along the way to reflect on the ministry of Jesus. And in verses 11-13, he does just that! It may be that these words were taken from a Christian hymn, or possibly Paul penned them himself as he wrote these words to Timothy. Reflect on each couplet of this hymn, and the incredible security of the Christian faith:

"For if we died with Him,

_____;

If we endure,

_____;

If we deny Him,

_____;

If we are faithless,

_____;

_____."

2nd Timothy 2

3. What was it important for Timothy to do for his congregation, according to verse 14a?

"These things" would be all the things Paul has been entrusting to Timothy by way of instruction, but perhaps especially the reminder to, *"Remember Jesus Christ!"*

   a. What charge was Timothy to give his congregation, and why?

Paul tells Timothy to charge them *before the Lord*. Before God, they were to forsake the useless and potentially harmful activity of arguing over words. The gospel message was so pure and so simple—that is what they were to keep as the center of their attention.

4. Rather than arguing over unimportant details or having foolish discussions, Paul tells Timothy to be diligent to do *certain* things. From verse 15:

✣ *To present himself to God in what manner?*

✣ *To be what kind of a worker?*

✣ *To handle the word of God in what way?*

5. In verses 17 and 18, Paul mentions two men who apparently were <u>not</u> diligent in handling the word of truth and who did not avoid the kind of discussions that lead to ungodliness. What were their names, what were they teaching, and what was the result of this teaching?

This teaching was most likely influenced by the Greek philosophy that the body was evil; therefore, according to their thoughts, resurrection was not of the body itself, but was spiritual and took place at salvation. This application of the resurrection was a sort of combined effort—taking some truth and mingling it with their own belief system so as to make sense to them. The problem with this is that the bodily resurrection of Christ is essential to the Christian faith, and the future promise of bodily resurrection is the Christian's hope.

    a. What does 1 Corinthians 15:12-14 teach us about the importance of the doctrine of resurrection?

    b. How does 2 Corinthians 4:14 present this as our hope?

It is clear to us why this false teaching on the resurrection would upset the faith of some of those who listened. It is also clear why we are not to listen to anyone's own thoughts or philosophies, but only to the teachings that are found in Scripture.

6. Paul begins verse 19 with the word, *nevertheless*. In other words, *although* this teaching has been given and even upset the faith of some, it will not last, and it will not prevail. Why is this, according to verse 19?

Review this week's memory verse.

Day 3
Read 2 Timothy 2:20-26

Once again, the message becomes personal to Timothy and to us, as Paul paints a picture of vessels both to honor and to dishonor. John MacArthur shows the flow in 2 Timothy 2 to be from the call to be "strong in the grace that is in Christ Jesus" (v. 1), to being "a worker who does not need to be ashamed" (v. 15), in order to be "useful for the Master, prepared for every good work" (v. 21).

1. Name the different kinds of vessels listed in verse 20. Which of these vessels would be considered vessels for honor and which would be vessels for dishonor? Which of these do you desire to be?

2. From the thoughts that follow in verse 21, see if you can describe the vessel for honor.

   a. The word sanctified means to be *set apart*. Can you say that you are a person who is set apart—in other words, you are not just one of the crowd (the world) but see yourself as set apart for God and His purposes? What does Psalm 4:3 tell us?

   b. Is it your desire to be useful to the Master? How would you like to do this?

The word prepared (for every good work) is *hetoimazo,* which has the idea of willingness and eagerness as well as readiness. Are you *prepared* for every good work?

    c. What does Ephesians 2:10 tell you about our good works? Are you walking in such a way that you will naturally be *prepared* for those good works?

Paul says, *"If anyone cleanses himself from the latter, he will be a vessel for honor."* There are different thoughts on the meaning of *the latter* (*these things,* NASB). Most likely it refers to the false teachings; verse 16 may very well be the reference point of these words.

3. From what is Timothy to flee? v. 22

    a. What might some *youthful lusts* be? Do you need to take heed to this word?

    b. What is he to pursue?

    c. With whom is he to pursue these virtues? What does this mean to you?

4. What is Timothy to avoid and why? v. 23

2nd Timothy 2

This is a continuation of Paul's theme of avoiding arguing about unimportant details and having foolish discussions. The last three verses of this chapter are tied to this thought.

5. What four things does Paul say about the one who calls himself a servant of the Lord? v. 24

He must_____.
He must_____.
He must_____.
He must_____.

   a. How is God's servant to correct those who are in opposition? See 2 Timothy 2:25a; Titus 3:2; and Galatians 6:1

   b. When the Lord's servant acts in the manner prescribed, what is the hopeful outcome?

   verse 25

   verse 26

This certainly puts the responsibility of properly handling correction into the proper perspective! Notice that Paul speaks of God *granting* them repentance. Romans 2:4 tells us that it is the *goodness* of God that leads to repentance and Titus 3:4 speaks of the kindness of God our Savior!

6. Are you careful in your manner toward others, knowing that you are the Lord's servant (or as Mary put it, *handmaiden*)? Do you need to work on any of the areas mentioned in verses 24-25? Name an area of need here and ask someone who you can trust to pray for your growth in this way.

Review this week's memory verse.

Day 4
Overview of 2 Timothy 2

Today we will be looking at the passage we have studied this week as a whole. The goal is to find the main lessons the Lord has for us from this chapter. Don't worry about being clever or profound—just do your best!

Find the Facts ...

1. See if you can state the *content* of this week's passage in a couple of sentences. (Who is speaking, what is taking place, what is the main subject?)

Look for the Heart ...

2. What do you think is the main *lesson* of this passage? (What spiritual truths are taught here? Is there a command to obey, a warning to heed, a promise to claim?)

Hear Him Speak...

3. Look for a *personal application* from the content of this passage. It should come from the lesson you got from the chapter (question 2). How will you apply the lesson to yourself?

4. Was there a particular verse that ministered to you this week? What was it and how did it minister to you?

5. Write out your memory verse *from memory*!

NOTES

2 TIMOTHY 3

Our passage this week deals, once again, with the subject of apostasy. At first glance, as we read these verses, it would seem that Paul is describing the world at large, a description at which we are not surprised as we consider the state of affairs in the world today. But actually, Paul is speaking here of church leaders—apostate church leaders. 1 Timothy 4:1 tells us that *"in latter times some will fall away from the faith."* The latter times are the period of time from the first coming of Christ until He returns. We can't help but think of our own times when we read these words, as it seems evident that we are very near to the second coming of Christ. The word for *fall away* (1 Timothy 4:1) means *to depart from,* or *to remove oneself from the position originally occupied to another place.* It speaks of those who come very close to the truth of salvation, only to abandon that position or leave. The apostate that Paul describes in chapter 3, then, is a rejecter of Christ *from within the ranks of the church.*

Day 1
Read 2 Timothy 3:1-9

1. What revelation does Paul make in verse 1 about the last days?

The word *perilous* in the NKJV is translated *difficult* in the NASB and *terrible* in the NIV. It means *dangerous, hard to deal with, savage*.

  a. *Digging Deeper:* Speaking specifically of the end times, Matthew 24:4-14 tells us several things. These words were spoken by Jesus in answer to his disciples' questions about the end of the age. Read these verses and share some of the specific things which will take place.

  b. Do you recognize any of these things as already beginning to take place? What does that tell you?

  c. Are we to be afraid of these things? Matthew 24:6 Why?

2. In 2 Timothy 3:2-4, Paul gives eighteen characteristics of "men" in these (latter) times. List them here.

  a. What does Matthew 24:12 say about the end times that agrees with what you see here?

b. Do the characteristics mentioned in these verses sound familiar? List some that you see as evident today.

c. How does he describe the religion of these men? v. 5

d. What is Timothy to do about or with them? v. 5b

From verse 5, we understand that Paul is speaking of *religious* men who hold a *form* (outward shape and appearance) of godliness but deny the true power of God. A good example of such men is the Pharisees, as seen in the gospels.

3. Read **Matthew 23:25-28** for Jesus' words of woe to the religious leaders of His day—who looked very pious but were spiritually bankrupt.

   a. What did He say they were like? v. 27

   b. How did He describe their condition? v. 28

   c. What was His prescription for them? v. 26

4. What is the *power* of the Christian's faith, and why do the merely *religious* leaders not have this power? 1 Corinthians 1:18

5. Paul makes some specific statements about the sin of these false church leaders. What does he say some of them are known to do? 2 Timothy 3:6

The women spoken of in this verse seem to be women who have some desire for truth but are weak, ungrounded in the Word, evidently having no real faith to believe and receive forgiveness for their sins, and who are led by their desires rather than by the Spirit of God.

   a. What does Paul say about their spiritual education? v. 7

   b. Share some thoughts as to why a person might be *always learning and never able to come to the knowledge of the truth.*

   c. Have you known anyone like this? What might be some ways in which you could help them?

6. Paul uses Jannes and Jambres (believed to be the Egyptian magicians who attempted to counterfeit Moses' miracles) as an example of the false teachers in Ephesus. How does he describe them and all who lead others astray? v. 8

a. Will these men prevail? v. 9

b. *Digging Deeper:* Follow the downward spiral of Jannes and Jambres by reading Exodus 7:10-12, 8:6-7, 8:17-18, and 9:10-11.

This week's memory verse: "Be imitators of me, just as I also am of Christ." 1 Corinthians 11:1

Day 2
Read 2 Timothy 3:10-12

Paul now turns his thoughts, in sharp contrast, from the description of the apostate leaders, to Timothy, himself.

1. What does Paul say here that Timothy had the opportunity to do through his years with Paul? v. 10

    a. Look up the following verses, which define Paul's direction in each of these areas:

    ⚜ *His doctrine*—1 Corinthians 2:2

    ⚜ *His manner of life*—1 Corinthians 11:1

✣ *His purpose*—Acts 20:24; 1 Corinthians 9:16b; Philippians 3:10

✣ *His faith*—2 Timothy 1:12

✣ *His longsuffering*—1 Thessalonians 5:14; 1 Corinthians 13:4a

✣ *His love*—Romans 9:3

✣ *His perseverance*—2 Timothy 2:8-9

2. How does 1 Corinthians 4:17 emphasize the fact that Timothy knew the *ways* of the apostle Paul?

    a. How does 1 Corinthians 4:16 sum up the idea behind Paul's words in 2 Timothy 3:10

3. What else had Timothy followed according to verse 11?

2nd Timothy 3

    a. What persecutions had Paul suffered at Antioch? Acts 13:50

    b. What persecutions had Paul suffered at Iconium? Acts 14:4-6

    c. What persecutions had Paul suffered at Lystra? Acts 14:19

    d. *Digging Deeper:* For greater detail of Paul's persecutions and sufferings read 2 Corinthians 11:24-33.

4. What prediction does Paul make in verse 12 which applies to *all who desire to live godly in Christ Jesus* including Timothy, and including us?

    a. Why might this be? John 15:18-20; 1 John 3:1b

    b. What charge are we given by Jesus in Matthew 16:24? How does Matthew 10:38 finish this thought?

5. Following Christ may bring persecution from the world and even a degree of suffering, as we are touched by the Cross in our own lives, but what is Paul's hopeful testimony in 2 Corinthians 4:8-9?

Is this your testimony in your place of trial today?

   a. Finish Paul's thoughts from 2 Timothy 3:11b: *"What persecutions I endured. And _____ _____."*

   b. Do you believe the Lord can and <u>will</u> deliver you out of the trouble or dilemma you are in today? See Psalm 34:19 for encouragement.

Review this week's memory verse.

Day 3
Read 2 Timothy 3:13-17

1. In verses 13 and 14, we have another contrast between Timothy and the false teachers: What will the course of the apostates be? v. 13

   a. What course will Timothy follow? v. 14

2. Notice Paul speaks of things Timothy has learned and become *assured* of. What does it mean to be *assured* (*convinced*, NASB) of something?

   a. Are you *assured* of the things which you have been learning as you study God's Word? Why is it important that we are personally assured of the teachings of God's Word?

3. From whom had Timothy been learning these things? 2 Timothy 1:13; 3:10

   a. Timothy was Paul's disciple. He had followed Paul's doctrine, manner of life, purpose, etc. Is there anyone special who God has brought into *your* life to teach you and model for you the Christian life and walk?

   b. Is there anyone God has given you the opportunity to disciple—someone for whom you are a model of the Christian way of life? If not, would you like the opportunity to do this? Pray and ask God to bring someone along for you to disciple. It will be another opportunity for you to put your faith into action.

c. Read 1 Corinthians 11:1. From this verse, why was Paul able to tell the Corinthians to be imitators of him? Do you recognize this as a pre-requisite for discipleship? Share your thoughts.

4. What had Timothy known since childhood, according to verse 15?

Many Christians have dramatic testimonies of turning from a life characterized by sin after finding Jesus, His forgiveness, and salvation. Some Christians, like Timothy, have the wonderful testimony of being *raised* in the Word and in the admonition of the Lord.

a. Do you remember who had shared with Timothy the words of wisdom which led to his salvation? How did you come to know Jesus Christ as *your* Savior?

In verse 15, we see that it is the *Holy Scriptures* that lead to salvation through faith in Jesus Christ.

5. What does verse 16 tell us about the *origin* of Scripture? What do you think this means?

a. Notice that this verse says that *all* Scripture is inspired by God. Do you believe this? What does this mean to you?

6. Verse 16 also tells us that all Scripture is *profitable*. What is the Word of God able to do for us?

    a. Are you allowing the Word of God to do this kind of work in your life? What will be the outcome for you *personally* as you read, meditate on, and study God's Word? (v. 17)

"I will be_____."

    b. 2 Timothy 2:21b speaks of us being *"a vessel for honor, sanctified and useful for the Master, prepared for every good work."* How do our verses today show you the way to become that vessel for honor?

Is this your heart's desire? If it is, then by being diligent and trusting the Lord, you may be sure that it will come to pass!

"Delight yourself in the Lord; and He will give you the desires of your heart. Commit your way to the Lord, trust also in Him, and He will do it." Psalm 37:4-5

Review this week's memory verse.

Day 4
Overview of 2 Timothy 3

Today we will be looking at the passage we have studied this week as a whole. The goal is to find the main lessons the Lord has for us from this chapter. Don't worry about being clever or profound—just do your best!

Find the Facts...

1. See if you can state the *content* of this week's passage in a couple of sentences. (Who is speaking, what is taking place, what is the main subject?)

Look for the Heart...

2. What do you think is the main *lesson* of this passage? (What spiritual truths are taught here? Is there a command to obey a warning to heed, a promise to claim?)

Hear Him Speak...

3. Look for a *personal application* from the content of this passage. It should come from the lesson you got from the chapter (question 2). How will you apply the lesson to yourself?

4. Was there a particular verse that ministered to you this week? What was it and how did it minister to you?

5. Write out your memory verse *from memory*!

NOTES

2 TIMOTHY 4

Chapter 4 of 2 Timothy contains the final *charge*, *testimony*, and *farewell* of Paul the apostle to his beloved Timothy; as well as the last of his inspired writings. Paul knew his life was soon to end, but he had no regrets, because he knew he had accomplished what God had committed to him and he knew he was bound for heaven!

"But none of these things move me; nor do I count my life dear to myself, so that I may finish my race with joy, and the ministry which I received from the Lord Jesus ..."
Paul, Acts 20:24

Day 1
Read 2 Timothy 4:1-5

1. Paul begins his final thoughts to Timothy with a charge—a *solemn* charge. In whose presence does Paul make this charge?

There is an accountability factor in the way Paul begins his thoughts.

Paul, in a sense, reminds Timothy that he stands in the presence of God and Christ Jesus and it is to *Him* that he is accountable for his ministry.

    a. To which aspect of Christ's ministry does Paul point in this verse?

    b. Of what judgment is Paul speaking here? 2 Corinthians 5:10

    c. When will this judgment take place? (v. 1)

2. The charge Paul gives Timothy consists of nine specific commands; five of them are found in verse 2. What are they?

    a. The first command is *to preach*. The word preach means *to herald or to proclaim publicly*. What is Timothy to preach?

    b. Why is it important that the minister preach the Word of God—not simply his own thoughts or experiences? See 2 Timothy 3:15-16

    c. Why is preaching the Word the most important ministry of the pastor? Romans 10:14 and 17

3. The second command is that Timothy be ready (or instant) in season and out of season. What do you think this might mean?

   a. Ephesians 5:15-16 helps us get an understanding of Paul's words here. What does it say?

   b. Are you ready to serve God whether the moment *seems* opportune or not? Are you making the most of your time? How can you be ready in season and out? (1 Timothy 4:15-16 may be helpful.)

The next three commands—convince, rebuke, and exhort—are of a similar nature. *Convince* is translated *correct* in NIV and *reprove* in NASB. Reproof—*elegmos*—carries the idea of correcting misbehavior or false doctrine. While reproof speaks of correction, *rebuke*, a similar word, speaks of bringing a person under conviction and toward repentance. *Exhort* has a more positive meaning, and carries the idea of encouragement.

4. As difficult as it may be, the pastor, as well as other Christian leaders, is duty-bound to reprove, rebuke, and exhort. Why is it important for the church that the pastor and other leaders be willing to discharge this unpleasant task?

a. How is this task to be done? v. 2b Why is it important that it be done in this way?

b. Why is it important that exhortation (encouragement) be included with reproof and rebuke? How might you go about encouraging a person you are correcting?

5. How do verses 3 and 4 explain the necessity for Timothy to take heed to Paul's charge?

a. What do you think these words mean: *"because they have itching ears, they will heap up for themselves teachers?"*

Four more commands, or charges, follow in verse 5. In contrast with those who will turn aside from the truth, Paul says, once again, *"But you ..."*

✣ *Be watchful in all things ...* Being watchful (sober, NASB) means being level-headed, well ordered, and in control. NIV translates it "keep your head."

✣ *Endure afflictions ...* Woven throughout all of 2 Timothy is the factor of *certain* hardship for the one who will faithfully serve his Master. Paul is Timothy's example in this.

✣ *Do the work of an evangelist* ... As a preacher and teacher of God's Word, a most significant part of Timothy's ministry would be proclaiming the Good News of salvation in Jesus Christ.

✣ *Fulfill your ministry* ... The word fulfill—*plerophoreo*—means giving full measure, bringing to completion. In relation to work, it carries the idea of eagerness and wholeheartedness. This word is not only the last of the nine commands given—but Paul's last written charge to Timothy.

✣ Why is the final command to Timothy—*fulfill your ministry*—a perfect summation to all that Paul has charged him?

   a. The definition of the word *fulfill,* in Paul's charge to Timothy, speaks of eagerly and wholeheartedly bringing to completion the ministry God has given. How can *you* apply this charge to your own life and ministry (or service to the Lord)?

This week's memory verse: "I press on toward the goal for the prize of the upward call of God in Christ Jesus." Philippians 3:14

Day 2
Read 2 Timothy 4:6-8

As Paul finishes writing his final charge to Timothy with the words *fulfill your ministry*, he turns his thoughts back to his own life and ministry that he knows is coming to an end. These verses could be seen as Paul's epitaph, as Paul considers his *present*, his *past,* and his *future* ...

1. How does Paul describe his *present* circumstances in verse 6?

A drink offering consisted of wine poured out on an altar as a sacrifice to God.

   a. In Romans 12:1, Paul speaks of the Christian's life as a sacrifice to God. What does he direct us to do here?

Paul sees his life as a *living sacrifice* and his death as a *drink offering* poured out to his Lord and God in a final act of service and submission. In every way, since being called on that road to Damascus, Paul's life was abandoned to God.

2. What were Paul's views on life and death according to Philippians 1:21?

   a. How does Philippians 1:23 show that Paul was not afraid of death?

2nd Timothy 4

These words to the Philippians were written during Paul's first Roman imprisonment. Now, during his second and final imprisonment, Paul says, *"The time of my departure is at hand."*

3. In reflecting *back* over his life and ministry, what three faith-filled statements did Paul make? v. 7

1.
2.
3.

   a. Looking at his life as a race—how had Paul run this race, and what was his focal point? Hebrews 12:1-2

   b. How does Paul describe his attitude in Philippians 3:13b-14?

4. Paul gives another picture of the race in 1 Corinthians 9:24-27. From these verses:

✣ How had Paul run his race? v. 26a

✣ How had he fought the fight? v. 26b

✣ How did he make certain he wasn't disqualified?

a. What, again, did this diligent labor and purposeful living enable him to say at the end of his life? 2 Timothy 4:7

b. Considering the verses we have just looked at, are there any changes that you need to make in your own life in order to have peace and no regrets when your time on this earth is over?

5. As he looked toward the *future*, of what was Paul certain? 2 Timothy 4:8

Notice *who* Paul pictured as the One who would present him with this crown—Jesus Christ, the *righteous* judge—the One whom he had met so many years earlier on that Damascus Road. Think of what that reunion would have been like!

a. In this verse, Paul holds out this same promise to all believers. What does he say is the condition for this reward? v. 8b

The word "appearing" doesn't speak of Christ's second coming but of the rapture of the church, when we will be *caught up* to meet the Lord in the air to be with Him always. Are you looking forward to that heavenly appointment? There is a crown of righteousness waiting for those who are!

Review this week's memory verse.

Day 3
Read 2 Timothy 4:9-22

In the final thoughts of this letter, Paul speaks of many who are friends and some who are not and adds a final note of appreciation to the Lord, who has faithfully seen him through.

1. What was it Paul's desire that Timothy soon be able to do? v. 9

    a. How had Paul already revealed his longing to see Timothy, in 2 Timothy 1:3-4?

    b. When did he hope for Timothy to come? v. 21

    c. What did Paul want Timothy to bring? v. 13

Paul knew that his days were numbered and that it would take time for this letter to reach Timothy and for Timothy to reach Rome. He also saw the difficult winter approaching and knew he would need his cloak for warmth and his books for study.

Isn't it interesting that Paul was a student until the end? He could certainly have let that go in his final days—but he was a scholar, a preacher, a teacher, and a writer at heart—all the way until the end!

2. *Digging Deeper:* Of the people mentioned in this passage, Demas, Luke, and Mark are spoken of in Philemon 23-24, Demas and Luke in Colossians 4:14, and Mark again in Colossians 4:10. Comparing these verses with 2 Timothy 4:10, what seems to have happened to Demas?

Although Demas' name is mentioned in the same verse with Crescens and Titus, it does not follow that the latter two had also left the faith. They had simply moved on to new places of ministry.

Luke, referred to by Paul as *beloved physician,* is the author of both the gospel that bears his name and the book of Acts. Any time you see the word *we* recorded in Acts 16-28, it is inclusive of Luke.

    a. What does verse 11 tell us about Luke now?

There is a true sense of Paul's loneliness in the words of this verse. We see again how he must have longed for Timothy's presence. As a side note, it is very possible that Luke was the one to whom Paul dictated this letter.

3. *Digging Deeper:* Mark, spoken of in verse 11, is *John* Mark, the author of the gospel of Mark. Acts 13:1-3, 5, 13; 15:36-41; Colossians 4:10; and 1 Peter 5:13 give us an account of his ministry. See if you can follow his path through these verses.

2nd Timothy 4

a. Here we see Paul speak of Mark as being *useful for service*. What can we learn from Mark's example?

Verse 12 tells us that Paul has sent Tychicus to Ephesus. It is thought that: 1) Tychicus was probably the one through whom this letter was sent to Timothy, and 2) Tychicus would likely have taken Timothy's post as he left to visit Paul.

4. What did Alexander the coppersmith do? v. 14

Paul could do nothing personally to stop Alexander (who it is thought may have testified against him in Rome), but he sees that God would repay him according to his deeds. Just as God would *reward* Paul for his work, He would also deal justly with Alexander for his.

a. See Paul's own words as to the believer's proper position in the matter of repaying a wrong. Romans 12:17-19

b. What warning did he give Timothy about this man? v. 15

5. *Digging Deeper:* Other names that come up are Prisca (Priscilla) and Aquila, devoted friends of Paul. What do you learn about them from Acts 18:25-26; Romans 16:3-4; and 1 Corinthians 16:19?

a. Once again, we see the name Onesiphorus. What had Paul said about him in 2 Timothy 1:16-18?

b. What do we learn about Erastus in Acts 19:22?

c. What do we learn about Trophimus in Acts 20:4; 21:29?

We know nothing about Eubulus, Pudens, Linus, or Claudia, except that they were obviously part of the Roman church and possibly part of the number who deserted Paul in his first defense.

6. What does Paul say about his *first defense* in verse 16?

   a. How did he show his willingness to forgive? v. 16b

   b. All in Rome may have deserted him, but who stood by him and strengthened him? v. 17 Why?

   c. What two words of hope does Paul continue to have? v. 18

Paul couldn't lose, and neither can we if we learn to take these thoughts to heart! If we are called to ministry in the service of the Lord, then we can be sure that He will be faithful to us (*utterly faithful* according to 1 Thessalonians 5:24, Phillips translation) and that He will stand by us and strengthen us so that we can *fulfill our ministry*.

Paul sees himself as delivered out of the lions mouth, delivered from every evil work, and safely on his way to heaven!

    d. What are Paul's final words in this letter to Timothy—and to those of us who are part of the body Christ? v. 22

Review this week's memory verse.

Day 4

Overview of 2 Timothy 4

Today we will be looking at the passage we have studied this week as a whole. The goal is to find the main lessons the Lord has for us from this chapter. Don't worry about being clever or profound— just do your best!

Find the Facts...
1. See if you can state the *content* of this week's passage in a couple of sentences. (Who is speaking, what is taking place, what is the main subject?)

Look for the Heart...

2. What do you think is the main *lesson* of this passage? (What spiritual truths are taught here? Is there a command to obey, a warning to heed, a promise to claim?)

Hear Him Speak...

3. Look for a *personal application* from the content of this passage. It should come from the lesson you got from the chapter (question 2). How will you apply the lesson to yourself?

4. Was there a particular verse that ministered to you this week? What was it and how did it minister to you?

5. Write out your memory verse *from memory*!

NOTES

TITUS 1

The letter to Titus is the third part of the series known as the Pastoral Epistles. It was written by the apostle Paul, most likely around AD 64 or 65, sometime after he wrote 1 Timothy and a year or so before his final letter, 2 Timothy, was written. It seems possible that, after Paul's release from his first Roman imprisonment, he traveled with Titus to Crete where he left Titus to oversee the existing churches. The purpose of this letter is much the same as the purpose for Paul's letters to Timothy: to encourage, strengthen, and instruct him in his difficult ministry to Crete, as well as to give him the authority, as Paul's representative there, to carry out what was needed to be done. Paul's words in Titus 1:5, *"For this reason I left you in Crete, that you might set in order the things that are lacking, and appoint elders in every city as I commanded you,"* relate Paul's direction for the ministry of Titus in Crete. In this letter, Paul focuses on the qualifications of church leaders, the character and conduct of church members, and the character and conduct of both the leaders and members of the church before an unbelieving world.

Titus 1

Day 1
Read Titus 1:1-4

Paul always begins his letters with opening greetings. This particular greeting is quite lengthy, actually one very long sentence with many important thoughts, which clearly define Paul's ministry of the gospel message and hope.

1. Paul begins by identifying himself in two ways, what is the first way? v. 1

The word for servant, *doulos,* is often translated *slave.*

   a. Romans 6:20-22 speaks of slavery to sin and slavery to God. What concept does it give of the latter? (v. 22)

   b. What important point does 1 Corinthians 6:20 make?

   c. How does 2 Corinthians 5:15 sum up this perspective most beautifully?

Paul was a man who could have been prideful and insistent upon controlling his own destiny, rather than submitting his life, plans, future, and and purpose to God.

2. **Philippians 3:4-8** gives us Paul's views concerning those things in which he had formerly put his confidence. Read these verses and answer the following:

a. Why was it that Paul *could* have had confidence in the flesh? (vv. 4-6)

b. Rather than having confidence in himself and his religious upbringing, how did Paul perceive these past achievements? (v. 7)

c. How does Philippians 3:8 clearly reveal Paul's love and submission to his Lord?

3. Who was Paul's supreme example of a servant? See Philippians 2:5-8

a. In a word, what was the final outcome of this One? Philippians 2:9

b. What does 1 Peter 5:6 show to be the outcome of all who submit humbly to God?

4. What is the second way Paul identified himself in verse 1?

We have seen Paul identify himself in this manner in both of his letters to Timothy. The word "apostle" means *one who is sent* and carries the basic meaning of *messenger*.

    a. Who is Paul a messenger of, according to this verse?

The NLT translates verses 1-3 in this way:

¹"This letter is from Paul, a slave of God and an apostle of Jesus Christ. I have been sent to bring faith to those God has chosen and to teach them to know the truth that shows them how to live godly lives. ²This truth gives them the confidence of eternal life, which God promised them before the world began—and he cannot lie. ³And now at the right time he has revealed this Good News, and we announce it to everyone. It is by the command of God our Savior that I have been trusted to do this work for him."

5. From verse 1 NLT, what was the purpose for which Paul was sent (2 reasons)?

    a. What is the *hope* of the message Paul has been entrusted to carry? How can he be sure of this hope? v. 2 NLT (Does this thought give you hope?)

    b. What would Paul do with this Good News he had received? v. 3a NLT

c. What, in a nutshell, was the message Paul was to proclaim? 1 Corinthians 15:3-4

6. In addressing this letter to Titus, what does Paul call him? v. 4 What would this signify?

   a. *Digging Deeper:* Read the following verses from 2 Corinthians to get a glimpse of this man, Titus, his relationship with (and ministry to) Paul, as well as his ministry at Corinth: 2:13; 7:5-7, 13-14; 8:6, 16-17, 23; 12:18.

Titus was also Paul's case in point that circumcision was unnecessary to those saved by grace. Titus was not Jewish; he was a Gentile—Greek by birth, so therefore uncircumcised. The false message, which Paul made it his purpose to refute, was that believers in Christ must still be circumcised according to the Old Testament law. Paul said "Not so!" and Titus was his example (see Galatians 2:3-5).

   b. How did Paul greet Titus in this letter?

This week's memory verse: "For you have been bought with a price: therefore glorify God in your body." 1 Corinthians 6:20

Titus 1

Day 2
Read Titus 1:5-9

1. For what 2 reasons had Paul left Titus in Crete?

There seem to be fifteen qualifications for eldership mentioned in this passage. The first three are found in verse 6.

2. What is the first qualification Paul names for the would-be elder? v. 6a

The word blameless—*anenkletos*—carries the idea of being above reproach. Of course, we know that no one is perfect, but the one who is considered for eldership must live a life that is in accordance with what he professes to believe.

   a. How does Paul's charge to Timothy in 1 Timothy 4:12 point him to a life which is above reproach? Is this the life you are endeavoring to live?

   b. What is the second qualification mentioned in verse 6?

In naming this qualification, Paul is not referring to polygamy—that is obviously wrong; nor is he prohibiting remarriage after the death of a spouse—that, of course, would be acceptable. He is speaking of marital faithfulness.

The man chosen to be elder must have a reputation for devotion and purity concerning his marriage.

    c. What is the final qualification in this verse? What do you think this means?

It is an understandable qualification for leading the church that a man be able to lead his family.

In the next group of qualifications, Paul begins by reiterating the fact that the elder—here called bishop—must be above reproach. He follows with five negatives in verse 7 and six positives in verse 8.

3. List the five negative factors mentioned in verse 7 and answer the questions which follow each one:

✣ *He must not be:*

Was Paul self-willed? (Remember what we learned about him in the first day of our lesson?) Why does God not want you to be self-willed? What does he want you to be? See 1 Peter 5:5

✣ *He must not be:*

What harm is done by a quick-tempered person? For instruction on anger see James 1:19-20.

✣ *He must not be:*

What does too much wine do to a person's judgment? Why must the overseer not be addicted to wine?

✣ *He must not be:*

The meaning of Paul's phrase here is that he must not be a *fist fighter*. How does Paul make this same point in 2 Timothy 2:24-25?

✣ *He must not be:*

Should monetary gain (not provision, but gain) be the elder's purpose in serving the body of Christ? What type of ministry would someone have if they were "only in it for the money?"

4. What *is* this man to be? Titus 1:8

Many of these attributes are self-evident and have been previously discussed. We will look at only one—"a lover of what is good."

    a. Can you tell if a person is "a lover of what is good" simply by observing their life and actions? What would be the indicator that you love what is good in regard to the friends you choose, the books you read, the things you watch, the things you listen to, and the activities you're involved in?

b. How does the teaching in 2 Timothy 2:22 help us to go in the right direction?

5. What is the final qualification? v. 9a

This qualification, unlike the others that dealt with character, deals with the ministry of the elder. The elder could not run out on his own—he was to hold fast (strongly cling or adhere to) the faithful word—the very word of God that he had been taught.

a. What two things will this faithful word enable the elder to perform? (v. 9)

The pastor obviously has a two-fold ministry: to encourage the flock in the word of truth (sound doctrine) and to refute or speak out against those who came against that truth.

Review this week's memory verse.

Day 3
Read Titus 1:10-16

Once again, the subject of false teaching comes up—this time the offenders are in Crete.

1. In verse 10, what does Paul call these "offenders"?

Titus 1

These words are reminiscent of Paul's description of the false teachers in his letter to Timothy.

2. In speaking of the false teachers, what point, in particular, does Paul mention in verse 10b?

    a. What needs to be done with *these* men? v. 11a Why?

It seems that there were many Jews in the church of Crete; some who still believed that in order to be saved one must uphold the law of circumcision. Paul seemed to have a greater understanding than any that salvation is by grace alone—and that the one saved by grace is no longer under the law—including the law of circumcision. The silencing of this teaching would be an essential element of Titus' work in Crete.

3. In verse 12, Paul quotes a "prophet" of Crete (the poet, Epimenides), a man of their own, who intimately knew the character and type of people to whom Titus would be ministering. What did he say about them?

    a. What was Paul's evaluation of this statement? v. 13a

An interesting note is that an ancient phrase "to Cretanize" was used as a figure of speech for lying.

    b. What *must* Titus do, and why must he do it? vv. 13-14

4. Why is truth so important to the Christian? John 8:32

   a. How does Galatians 5:1 encourage us strongly to stay in the freedom the truth has brought?

   b. Of course, we know that Jesus Himself is the Truth, what does He say of Himself in John 14:6?

No one comes to the Father—*except by way of the Truth.*

   c. How does Proverbs 23:23 encourage us *toward truth?*

5. What does Paul say about the one who is pure? v. 15

   a. What about the one who is defiled and unbelieving?

   b. Though with their mouths they say they know God, how is their unbelief revealed? v. 16

   c. Are they capable of any good deeds, according to this verse?

Paul is speaking of men who "profess to know God;" professing believers who, according to verse 15, are really *unbelievers*.

Titus 1

Verse 16 brings us the very important issue of fruit. If someone is in the position of teaching you truth (your pastor and/or other spiritual teachers) then be sure that you see the fruit of the Spirit in their lives. The fruit of the Spirit is given in Galatians 5:22-23. Do you see this fruit developing in your own life?

Review this week's memory verse.

Day 4

Overview of Titus 1

Today we will be looking at the passage we have studied this week as a whole. The goal is to find the main lessons the Lord has for us from this chapter. Don't worry about being clever or profound—just do your best!

Find the Facts ...
1. See if you can state the *content* of this week's passage in a couple of sentences. (Who is speaking, what is taking place, what is the main subject?)

Look for the Heart ...
2. What do you think is the main *lesson* of this passage? (What spiritual truths are taught here? Is there a command to obey a warning to heed, a promise to claim?)

Hear His Voice ...

3. Look for a *personal application* from the content of this passage. It should come from the lesson you got from the chapter (question 2). How will you apply the lesson to yourself?

4. Was there a particular verse that ministered to you this week? What was it and how did it minister to you?

5. Write out your memory verse *from memory*!

NOTES

TITUS 2

In chapter 2, Paul gives Titus instructions for the behavior of the church. He gives him what we might call *patterns for holy living,* which are directly related to, and motivated by, the message of the gospel. *"For the grace of God that brings salvation has appeared to all men, teaching us that, denying ungodliness and worldly lusts, we should live soberly, righteously, and godly in the present age."* Find yourself in this passage and allow its message to penetrate your heart with God's desire and plan, in order that you might live godly in this present age.

Day 1
Read Titus 2:1-5

1. What type of people was Paul speaking about as we finished our study of chapter 1? Titus 1:15-16

    a. To whom is he speaking now? v. 1

Titus 2

    b. What instruction does he give?

2. What is appropriate for the older men, according to verse 2?

    a. The word reverent is translated "worthy of respect" in NIV. Share what it means to be a person worthy of respect.

    b. Why, for the body of Christ—and especially the younger men, is it important that the older Christian man be sober, reverent, temperate; sound in faith, love, and patience?

3. What is the appropriate behavior for the older Christian woman? v. 3

    a. The goal for the older woman is not simply *behaving* appropriately but being able, or in a position, to *teach* what is good. Why is personal example so important in teaching others?

4. List the seven things that the older women are to encourage the younger women to be and do. vv. 4-5

a. Considering the world in which we live today, why is it important that young women be *encouraged* to be and do these things?

b. What will be the result of the younger women taking heed to this encouragement? v. 5b

If you are a young woman today with a husband and small children, do you need to be encouraged in this way? It wouldn't seem to be necessary to teach a woman to love her husband, her children, or to be a keeper of her home, and yet we know that in reality these can be very difficult roles to fill. Take heart to the fact that the Lord knows that you need help in these areas and that He has provided you with this help in the form of older women who have learned through their own successes and failures, and who now have the advantage of hindsight to help them in encouraging you.

5. *For those who are married:* Share how you see yourself to be in need of encouragement in one or more of the following areas:

✟ *loving your husband—*

✟ *loving your children—*

✟ *working at home—*

✣ *being subject to your husband—*

    a. *For those who are either young and single or who are, in fact, one of the older women:* How might you be one who helps or encourages a young woman who is working to be obedient in these areas?

    b. *Whether married or single, young or old:* Read Proverbs 31:10-31 and share from your vantage point the benefits and blessings of being a godly wife, mother, and woman.

This week's memory verse: "And her children rise up and call her blessed; her husband also, and he praises her." Proverbs 31:28 NKJV

Day 2
Read Titus 2:6-10

1. Paul gives one word to the young men—what is it? v. 6

This word carries the idea of having common sense, good judgment, and self-control.

a. Considering that young men *marry* young women, how can this description give a sense of direction to the young woman who is waiting for the one the Lord has chosen for her in marriage?

b. If you are a young unmarried woman, are you looking for the man the *Lord* has chosen for you? What are you looking for in a young man? This verse (v. 6), along with 1 Timothy 3, should be of invaluable help to you in your pursuit!

c. If we think about the nature of young men to be impulsive, ambitious, passionate, and generally impatient, it is understandable that Paul would encourage them in this way. How did Paul encourage Timothy to handle *his* youthful impulses, and what did he encourage him to do instead? 2 Timothy 2:22

2. Titus himself is now encouraged by Paul. In what primary way does Paul encourage him? v. 7a

The word for pattern (example, NASB)—*tupos*—refers to a mark or impression left by an instrument. What type of a mark or impression would Titus, God's instrument, leave upon those to whom he ministered? What type of an impression do you leave upon those with whom you come into contact?

Titus 2

    a. In *how many things* was Titus to show himself a pattern of good works? v. 7a

Titus was ultimately the one to whom the people of Crete would look to see the gospel lived out. If it weren't possible for him, it most likely wouldn't be possible for them.

    b. In what specific areas was Titus to be an example? vv. 7-8

Can you see the benefit of taking Paul's direction in verses 7 and 8 for your own walk and behavior? Are you careful of the things you say and share about the Lord? Do you speak with purity of doctrine, realizing it is a holy God you serve? Do you conduct yourself in dignity—do you *respect* yourself? And do you speak in a manner that is above reproach, using *sound* speech or, according to the meaning of this word from which we get our word *hygiene*, using whole and healthy words?

    c. What would be the outcome of Titus' obedience in these areas? v. 8b

    d. Consider what the outcome of *your* obedience in these areas would be.

3. What five things was Titus to encourage those who were servants (slaves) to do? v. 9

4. Paul says they are to be subject to their masters in everything. Is there anyone to whom *you* need to willingly subject yourself as unto the Lord? What can you do today to begin to place yourself in submission to this one?

Submission is a difficult matter! It has always been and always will be, because there is a certain death of self involved. Yet, it is something that is required for men, women, children, those who are free, those who are not, the old, and the young. There is no way around it, and the quicker we learn it the better off we will be!

    a. Being well-pleasing goes together nicely with not being argumentative (answering back). Do you do your best to be pleasing to those around you, particularly those in authority over you, or are you more concerned that *they* please *you?*

    b. The word pilfering means *to put aside for oneself* and speaks of stealing by embezzlement. In other words, taking things little by little which have been entrusted to your care. It could be something as simple as taking office supplies from your work, or it could be as serious as lying on your time card and being paid for work you didn't do. What does Ephesians 4:28 tell us concerning this subject?

Titus 2

c. Showing all good fidelity refers to the valuable quality of loyalty. Do you have someone in your life who is loyal—one who is faithful and who you can count on? How about you, are you a loyal wife, mother, friend, relative, employee? This word speaks of being trustworthy, reliable, and utterly dependable. Is this something you could be called?

5. In the context of the slave, but in reality referring to *all* who have been mentioned in Paul's instructions, Paul gives the reason or purpose for calling them to holiness. What is it? v. 10b

    a. Does your life *adorn the doctrine of God your Savior in all things?* We have looked at many attitudes and behaviors in our lesson so far this week. Is there one area in which you have been convicted? If there is, share it here, and also share your thoughts as to how you will begin to work on that area today.

    b. Has God highlighted an area in your life in which you *are* living in accordance with the message you believe? Share that area here and how the Lord has helped you to bring that area into submission to Him and His will.

Review this week's memory verse.

Day 3
Read Titus 2:11-15

This passage has been entitled by someone, *Living in Response to God's Grace*. That is surely what this *whole chapter* is about. Paul has just given instruction to the older men and women, younger men and women, and finally to those in a position of slavery to live lives of holiness, so that they would adorn the doctrine of God. What is their motivation? It is God's grace.

1. What does verse 11 tell us about the grace of God?

    a. How does Titus 3:4 describe this appearance?

    b. What was this "appearance?" John 1:14; John 3:16

2. **Ephesians 2** gives us an in-depth look at the God of the *grace* spoken of in verse 11. Look at the verses listed from Ephesians 2 and share what you learn.

⁕ verses 4-5

⁕ verses 6-7

⁕ verse 8

It is impossible to look at these verses without seeing the depth of love God has for His creation. We see grace, kindness, love, and mercy, all directed *from* God *toward man*. Truly Ephesians 2:7 sums it up best: *"... so that in the ages to come He might show the surpassing riches of His grace in kindness toward us in Christ Jesus."*

3. Paul says that this very act of God's grace toward man in bring him salvation *teaches* us to do something. What is that? v. 12

   a. What is Paul basically telling us here?

   b. What is to be our focus and hope? v. 13

4. Paul speaks of Jesus as the one who gave Himself for us. How does Romans 5:6-8 describe this event?

5. In verse 14, Paul gives us two reasons why He did this, what is the first reason?

   a. How does Colossians 2:13-14 describe how this was accomplished?

b. Do your past sins haunt you? We see in Titus 2:14 that we no longer need to feel the weight of our sin—Jesus has redeemed us from every lawless deed! What is our part in this process? 1 John 1:9

c. How does Ephesians 1:7 beautifully describe what has taken place?

6. What is the second reason Jesus gave Himself for us? (v.14)

a. 1 Peter 2:9 gives us a lovely picture of who we are in Christ. What does it tell us?

b. What does 1 Peter 2:9b give as the destined outcome of our royal standing and relationship with Christ?

As we ponder the magnificence of what God has done for us through the sacrifice of His dear Son, the response will be two-fold: We will not only wish to *deny ungodliness and worldly lusts and live soberly, righteously and godly now,* but we will also desire to *proclaim the praises of Him who called us out of darkness and into His marvelous light!*

Review this week's memory verse.

Day 4
Overview of Titus 2

Today we will be looking at the passage we have studied this week as a whole. The goal is to find the main lessons the Lord has for us from this chapter. Don't worry about being clever or profound—just do your best!

Find the Facts ...

1. See if you can state the *content* of this week's passage in a couple of sentences. (Who is speaking, what is taking place, what is the main subject?)

Look for the Heart ...

2. What do you think is the main *lesson* of this passage? (What spiritual truths are taught here? Is there a command to obey, a warning to heed, a promise to claim?)

Hear His Voice ...

3. Look for a *personal application* from the content of this passage. It should come from the lesson you got from the chapter (question 2). How will you apply the lesson to yourself?

4. Was there a particular verse that ministered to you this week? What was it and how did it minister to you?

5. Write out your memory verse *from memory*!

NOTES

TITIUS 3

We come this week to the final chapter of Titus. The heart of this chapter is really the heart of the letter as a whole—that salvation by grace should manifest itself in good works. In other words, that belief results in behavior. Three times in this chapter we will see the exhortation to good works: verse 1, *"Remind them to ... be ready for every good deed;"* verse 8, *"... so that those who have believed God may be careful to engage in good deeds;"* and verse 14, *"And let our people also learn to engage in good deeds ..."*

Are you saved by the grace of Jesus Christ? What difference is your salvation making in the life that you now live? What would James tell us? *"... Faith without works is dead."*

Day 1
Read Titus 3:1-2

Paul begins this last chapter of Titus with the words *"Remind them."*

1. What was Titus to remind his congregation? vv. 1-2

a. Considering the intent of Paul in this letter tying behavior to belief, why was it important to Paul that Titus remind them of *these* things?

Paul is speaking here predominantly of the Christian's behavior among the non-believers rather than their brethren in Christ. These seven duties should characterize the believer's life. *Titus was to remind them to ...*

Be subject to rulers and authorities:
2. Why might we need to be *reminded* that it is God's will that we submit ourselves to the governing authorities over us?

   a. How does Romans 13:1 encourage us in this manner?

   b. In 1 Timothy 2:1-2, Paul went beyond the *attitude* of submission to the *heart* of the matter. What behavior did he encourage there?

   c. *Digging Deeper:* We get Jesus' heart on this matter in Matthew 22:15-22. Read this passage and share the counsel of Jesus in verse 21. What do you think this means?

Be obedient:
3. What is the only exception of our obedience to those in authority over us? See Acts 4:18-20 and 5:28-29.

Be ready for every good work:
4. What does Ephesians 2:10 teach us about our good works?

   a. What kind of Christian is ready for every good work? 2 Timothy 2:21 Are you this kind of *vessel?*

Speak evil of no one:
The NASB translates this phrase, *to malign no one.* The word malign—*blasphemeo*—gives us our word for blasphemy. It means to slander, curse, treat with contempt.

5. According to this verse, whom can we malign?

   a. Does this verse leave *any room* for slandering non-believers or treating them with contempt because they are not saved?

   b. What kind of an attitude do you have towards the lost? Do you feel superior to them because they are not saved? Is this an area you need to work on?

Be peaceable, gentle, showing all humility to all men:
The word *peaceable* means friendly and uncontentious, in contrast to being argumentative and quarrelsome. Gentle speaks of being moderate, fair, forbearing; another way of saying it might be "sweet reasonableness."

6. Remembering that we are predominantly speaking of our relationship to non-believers in this passage, describe how Paul wants us to behave toward them.

    a. Who is our example of humility and gentleness? Matthew 11:29

    b. 1 Corinthians 13:3-7 gives us the most beautiful example of true, Christian love. From these verses, share the attributes of Christ-like love.

This week's memory verse: "For God so loved the world, that He gave His only begotten Son, that whoever believes in Him shall not perish, but have eternal life." John 3:16

Day 2
Read Titus 3:3-7

Verses 3-7 continue to be a reminder to Titus' congregation.

First he is to remind them *how* to behave in a godly manner toward those who don't believe; now he reminds them *why:* *"For we ourselves were also once ..."*

1. What were we also once?

1.
2.
3.
4.
5.
6.
7.

    a. Were you *also once* any of these things? Does this reminder help you get some perspective on your dealings with non-believers?

Paul says, *"For we ourselves were also once ... But when ..."*

2. But when *what?* v. 4

    a. He did what? v. 5

For we were also disobedient once—but **He saved us!**

    b. Are you able to feel superior or contemptible toward non-believers when faced with this glorious fact? Why are you no longer like them?

Verses 4 and 5 show us what motivated God to save us. It was His *kindness*, His *love,* and His *mercy.* The word kindness—*chrestotes*—speaks of genuine goodness and generosity of heart. Love for mankind is *philanthropia*; *phileo* means to have affection for, and *anthropos* means man. Mercy—*eleos*—speaks of an outward manifestation of pity.

3. *Digging Deeper:* Psalm 103 is a lovely picture of God's love and compassion toward man. Read this Psalm and write down at least three places where you see his heart toward you. (My favorite verses in this Psalm are 4, 6, 13, 17 and 19!)

    a. See Isaiah 63:7-9 for another passage on the lovingkindness of our God.

4. Titus 3:4 and 5 not only show us what motivated God to save us, but they also show us what *did not.* What was *not* the basis of our salvation?

    a. What does Romans 3:10 tell us about righteousness?

    b. What does Isaiah 64:6 teach us about *our* righteousness?

    c. What is the only reason for our salvation, according to verse 5?

5. Now that we understand *why* we were saved, verse 5b tells us *how*. What does it say?

This work is done *by* the Holy Spirit, who was poured upon us abundantly at the time of our salvation through Jesus Christ our Savior!

    a. What does verse 7 add to these truths?

Salvation! The grand thought and plan and gift of God!

Before we were saved, we were foolish, disobedient, deceived, lustful, envious, and hateful--like every other sinner. But because of His kindness, love, and mercy, He saved us, by the washing of regeneration and renewing of the Holy Spirit.

6. *Digging Deeper:* Read Ezekiel 36:25-27 for a beautiful illustration of the *washing* we each received at the moment we were saved, as the Holy Spirit was richly poured out upon us.

Maybe you have come to this point in your study of God's Word and have not yet had this experience. Perhaps you are still in the filthiness of your sins and you realize today your need and great desire to be cleansed once and for all. Jesus Christ stands at the door of your heart at this very moment and knocks. All He asks you to do is recognize your need of Him and simply open the door so that He may come in and fellowship with you and you with Him.

It is at that moment when you open the door that all the wondrous things we have looked at in our study today will take place. At that instant you will be indwelt by the Holy Spirit who will cleanse you from all sin, you will be saved from the judgment that your sin deserves, you will be justified—or simply put, made *just as if you'd never sinned*, you will be made an heir with Christ, having the promise of eternal life. What could possibly keep you from bowing your heart before Him right now and asking Him to come in?

Review this week's memory verse.

Day 3
Read Titus 3:8-15

"This is a faithful saying ..." Once again, Paul uses this phrase to assure his readers that what he has just stated is a true statement worthy of their faith. In this instance, Paul is speaking of the long sentence in verses 4-7 in which he gave the basic gospel message. It is possible that he is also referring to everything he had said in chapter 2 and so far in chapter 3, emphasizing the believer's behavior.

1. What does Paul want Titus to do with this faithful saying? v. 8

Phillips translation says it this way: *"This is solid truth: I want you to speak about these matters with absolute certainty ..."*

    a. What difference does it make to your understanding and ability to believe when the one who teaches you speaks with absolute certainty?

b. This word from Paul is first to Titus, but truly it is for every believer to be able to share with absolute certainty the truth and reality of their salvation. How does 1 Peter 3:15 encourage us in this way?

2. What is the desired result for those who hear Titus' message? v. 8

Phillips translates it this way: "... *So that those who have believed in God may concentrate upon a life of goodness. Good work is good in itself and is also useful to mankind.*"

a. Have you believed in God? In other words, are you a born-again Christian? What, according to this translation, are you to *concentrate* on?

We concentrate on so many things in this life—what a wonderful direction this gives us to *remember* to concentrate on living a life of goodness.

b. Can we be self-centered and live this kind of life? What will we need to do?

The one thing that we can't miss here is that our good deeds are done out of a heart that has been saved by the grace and mercy of God.

Good deeds are always good and helpful to others, no matter who does them. But as Christians, we are motivated by the good that has first been done for us.

3. Once again, Paul brings up the false teachers. What is Titus to do with controversies and disputes about the law, and why? v. 9

4. Remember that the true gospel message is meaningless to those who are not truly born again and indwelt with the Holy Spirit. How does 1 Corinthians 1:18 say this?

   a. Shunning foolish controversies, what did Paul concentrate on in his message to those who were lost? 1 Corinthians 2:2

This does not mean that we don't confront wrong doctrine. Paul was a staunch defender of the gospel of grace, which was in stark contrast to the false teacher's *disputes about the law* (v. 9). But we may be sure that he didn't waste his time arguing the point with those who did not truly want to understand.

5. Along the same line of thought, what were they to do with a *factious* man, and why? vv. 10-11

The word factious speaks of one who is self-opinionated. In other words, one who places his opinions above the truth, refusing to consider viewpoints contrary to his own.

The thought here includes anyone in the church who is divisive and disruptive.

    a. Why do you think Paul allowed there to be a first and even second warning?

    b. Why, after the second warning, is Paul's direction to reject this one? See Romans 16:17-18

    c. How might you apply this warning of Paul's personally?

The last thoughts of this letter are personal words of Paul to Titus. It seems that it was Paul's plan for either Tychicus or Artemus to take over for Titus so that he could go to Paul in Nicopolis. Zenas and Apollos were most likely the ones who delivered this letter to Titus, Titus being encouraged to take care of their personal needs when they left him.

6. Paul's direction here is to *diligently* (NASB) help these men (Zenas and Apollos). What did Paul want accomplished for them? v. 13b

    a. Verse 14 continues on the same theme of good works, with this same motive in mind. What kinds of needs did Paul see the body of Christ helping with as they went about doing good works, and why?

b. *Digging Deeper:* Finish today's lesson by reading and meditating on the words of Jesus recorded in Matthew 25:31-46, in the passage we know as the "Sheep and the Goats." Be aware! This passage could make a lasting impression upon life as you know it!!!

Review this week's memory verse.

Day 4
Overview of Titus 3

Today we will be looking at the passage we have studied this week as a whole. The goal is to find the main lessons the Lord has for us from this chapter. Don't worry about being clever or profound—just do your best!

Find the Facts ...

1. See if you can state the *content* of this week's passage in a couple of sentences. (Who is speaking, what is taking place, what is the main subject?)

Look for the Heart ...

2. What do you think is the main *lesson* of this passage? (What spiritual truths are taught here? Is there a command to obey, a warning to heed, a promise to claim?)

Hear His Voice ...

3. Look for a *personal application* from the content of this passage. It should come from the lesson you got from the chapter (question 2). How will you apply the lesson to yourself?

4. Was there a particular verse that ministered to you this week? What was it and how did it minister to you?

5. Write out your memory verse *from memory*!

NOTES

ABOUT THE AUTHOR

Linda has dedicated her life to serving the Lord as a teacher, writer, and speaker. While teaching the Word of God, training leaders, and speaking at retreats and other women's ministry functions, she has also written curriculum for over 20 books of the Bible.

If you would be interested in having more information about her ministry or purchase her books/Bible Studies, please visit her blog at www.lindaosborne.net, or email her at myutmost1@aol.com.

www.ingramcontent.com/pod-product-compliance
Lightning Source LLC
Chambersburg PA
CBHW061644040426
42446CB00010B/1577